Dearest Gail,

This is a small "thank you" for all the fine effort you put into Relief Society in our old West Stanford III Branch. I appreciate and admire you a great deal!

A few thoughts to share with you— "He that is happy is happy still. We ought to learn to be happy right now, and find satisfaction in what we are doing right now, to live each day fully. We can't afford to sit around and wait for fulfillment. Fulfillment is a positive relationship with people —— now."

You're a good person and I love you for who you are and who you can become!

Love,
Ann

HOMESPUN

Domestic
Arts & Crafts
of Mormon
Pioneers

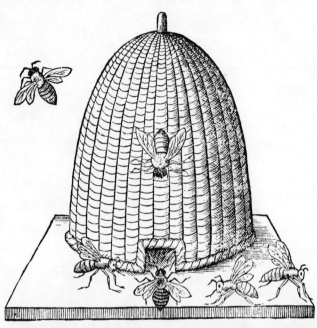

Shirley B. Paxman

HOMESPUN

Published by
Deseret Book Company
Salt Lake City, Utah
1976

To my mother,
Elsie Booth Brockbank,
who bridged the generation gap
with her homemaking skills.

PREFACE

Arts and crafts were a medium of expression for Mormon pioneers, just as they are for many persons today. In their search for freedom, the pioneers crossed the great plains to the western mountains, where they began to work their needles and shuttles, their looms and their lathes, in order to provide for their families' comfort and to create a corner of ordered beauty in the awesome West.

Many pioneer men and women came from the amenities of flourishing towns and cities to isolation on the frontier, where their conveniences and comforts were no longer available, and the struggle for survival became the motivating force in their lives. Out of their experience of the past, as well as from their native intelligence and determination to succeed, came the development of skills and crafts that blossomed into a life-style unique in history.

Many pioneers came from European centers of arts and crafts where they had learned their trades—in wood, iron, leather, textiles—as apprentices or guild members. They brought their knowledge with them, eager to use it in a new setting. They lacked tools, materials, and facilities, but in their new surroundings they gathered the necessities to begin again and to develop their arts and crafts to a new level of excellence.

A dozen "factories" were set up in pioneer kitchens. Women baked and brewed, washed and ironed, canned and pickled, compounded home remedies, carded, spun, wove, knit, quilted, made candles, soap, sausage, rugs, rag carpets, and featherbeds, and were in turn seamstresses, milliners, toymakers, and tailors.

As a pioneer mother wrote in her autobiography, "There was so much expected of the early frontier American woman: Candles and soap were made in the home; peaches were cut to dry; and fruit preserved in molasses. Mother learned to milk a cow when her housekeeping began in Utah." (Annie C. Tanner, *A Mormon Mother* [University of Utah Library, 1973], p. 4.) The spinning wheel and the loom were prominently placed in the earliest houses of logs or adobe and even in the rough dug-out shelter carved out of the side of a hill. When needed clothing and bedcoverings had been provided, the loom and spinning wheel were then turned to the production of articles of beauty for the home and its occupants.

It has been said that "art, to be a true national popular art, cannot be the art of experts; it must be a simple art produced by simple means and by artists who are not trained for special mastery." (Mary M. Atwater, *The Shuttlecraft Book of American Hand Weaving* [New York: Macmillan Co., 1951], p. 6.) Few of the pioneer women thought of themselves as "artists" or aspired to create a masterpiece. Most of them were content to express their joy in life in homely ways—by embroidering a beehive on a pinafore, or decorating table linen with a design from nature, such as a thistle, a grapevine, or a bird in flight; by canning and preserving; or by drying or pickling the fruits of their gardens.

Perhaps because these frontier women did not think of such everyday activities as art, they were marvelously unself-conscious about their work and therefore achieved more delightful results than they might have done if intimidated by rigid rules. When a woman took up her needle to do a piece of patchwork, some quilting, or embroidery, she was bound only by her imagination and the order imposed by the materials available.

Today many women are turning back to the arts and crafts of their pioneer ancestors to find joy in creating something for themselves and their families. They are discovering the happiness and satisfaction that come from making articles of beauty and practicality with their own hands.

There is also a new degree of relevance in seeking out these old-time skills and crafts, a relevance that has been brought about by ecological crises. The early pioneers were aware of the need to conserve their resources with the utmost care, and likewise today's women have become aware of their potential to provide attractive homes and to enrich their daily activities by resourcefully creating articles of aesthetic as well as practical beauty while conserving materials of the environment.

In gaining knowledge about these old-fashioned crafts with new application, we bridge the span across generations with the needle, the shuttle, the loom, the dye kettle, and, above all, with the inherent desire to create that is present in women of every age and time.

CONTENTS

CHAPTER ONE

LOG CABIN COOKING

Travel across the plains and mountains in covered wagons, pulling handcarts, or even on foot allowed for only primitive cooking, usually over an open fire and often scanty fuel. Families traveled fifteen to twenty miles a day, often eating cold stew, beans, or porridge three times a day.

All along those hundreds of miles of treacherous and difficult trail, the settlers carried the necessary supplies for survival. Food carried in the wagons had to be lightweight and nourishing and to keep well. When the supplies were gone, the pioneers wrested a living from the land. Their intuition plus their instinct for survival taught them to draw the best from the land in plant and animal nourishment. Impoverished, they learned to eat the tender sego-lily root, the nettle, and the various herbs and grasses that provided sustenance during the trek and early days of settlement.

The westward migrants usually began their journey with rations that included flour, bacon, and dried apples. The prices of food listed in St. Louis in 1847 give a clue to the kinds of provisions they carried: cornmeal, 25¢ a bushel; ginger, 11¢ a pound; lard, 3½¢ a pound; dried apples, 50¢ a bushel.

A recommended list of provisions for a family of five to equip them for the pioneer wilderness journey was published in the Nauvoo (Illinois) *Neighbor* on October 29, 1845. It included the following:

*1 good strong wagon box well covered
with a light box.*

*2 or 3 good yoke of oxen between
  the age of 4 and 10 years.*
2 or more milch cows.
1 or more good beefs.
3 sheep if they can be obtained.
*1000 lbs. of flour or other bread,
  or bread stuffs in good sacks.*
*1 good musket or rifle to each male
  over the age of twelve years.*
1 lb. powder.
4 lbs. lead . . . .
100 [lbs.] sugar
1 [lb.] cayenne pepper . . . .
½lb. mustard
10 [lbs.] rice for each family
1 [lb.] cinnimon
½ [lb.] cloves
1 doz. nutmegs.
25 lbs. salt
10 [lbs.] dried apples
1 bush. of beans
A few lbs. of dried beef or bacon.
5 lbs. dried peaches.
20 [lbs.] pumpkin
25 [lbs.] seed grain . . . .
20 lbs. of soap each family.
4 or 5 fish hooks and lines . . . .
*Cooking utensils to consist of bake kettle,
  fryingpan . . . .*
*Tin cups, plates, knives, forks, spoons,
  and pans as few as will do.*
*A good tent and furniture to each
  2 families.*
*Clothing and bedding to each family,
  not to exceed 500 pounds.*

(B. H. Roberts, *A Comprehensive History of the Church*, vol. 2, pp. 439-40.)

Methods of Cooking

The pioneers carried the food traditions from their past and adapted their favorite recipes to the primitive cooking conditions of an open campfire. One diary told of baking mince pies, bread, and meat over a campfire, using buffalo dung for fuel. On the trek westward, recipes were exchanged and improvised. Among the dishes mentioned in diaries and journals were potato pancakes, ginger cookies, and rusk (a cornmeal cereal). Other diaries mention johnnycakes, a simple cornmeal dish of mush formed into squares and baked over the campfire. The johnnycakes were split open and spread with pats of butter, which melted in the steamy hot bread. On cold mornings families were served hasty pudding with molasses for sweetening. This thick cornmeal pudding served as a stick-to-the-ribs porridge for all the family.

When settlements were established, preparation of meals became easier. In the earliest cabins, the kitchen was the largest room in the home. Such refinements as an open hearth or fireplace replaced the campfire, and later a roasting box was added—a metal box on legs with one side open to the fire. Still later came the improvised ovens of clay or brick, and then, the cookstove with a place for pots and pans as well as an oven. However, some elements of cooking remained primitive. Lacking precise measuring utensils, the housewife of pioneer days would add a "pinch of salt" or a "handful of sugar." Oven temperatures were tested by "feeling" the heat with a hand, and baked goods were pronounced done when they had a certain look as well as texture.

Information on how to salvage frozen potatoes, how to fatten turkeys ("they should be fed soft bricks broken into pieces with charcoal, also broken, and with six grains of corn per day"), and how to preserve hams, apples, and sweet potatoes were popular front-page articles in the newspapers of the day.

Correct procedures for milking cows were also given to the pioneer housewife. "If you would obtain all the milk from the cow you must treat her with the upmost gentleness; she must not stand trembling under your blows nor under your threats. She may at times need a little chastisement, but at such times you need not expect all her milk." (Mary K. Stout, "From a Nauvoo Pantry," *New Era*, December 1973, p. 43.)

Fresh Meat

Whenever possible, the basic supplies of the pioneer diet were supplemented by the fisherman or by the hunter who brought home pheasant and other game birds, squirrels, rabbits, deer, elk, or an occasional rattlesnake. Eliza R. Snow, a prominent pioneer woman and gifted writer, records the use of wild game during the trek:

... others ... do the general work of housekeeping and for our dinner send us a generous portion of their immense pot-pie; de-
signed to satisfy the hunger of about thirty stomachs. It is made of rabbits, squirrels, quails, prairie chickens, etc., the trophies of the success of our hunters, of which each division has its quota. Thus from time to time we are supplied with fresh meat which does much in lengthening out our flour. . . . (Diary of Eliza R. Snow, as quoted in Mabel Harmer, *The Story of the Mormon Pioneers*, 1943, p. 25.)

The meat, if sparse, was welcome and often extended by vegetables or stuffing. If any was left over, it was dried and kept for later use. An early pioneer weekly newspaper published a recipe for "Admiral Peacock's Pickle for Meat." The beef, after lying in brine ten weeks, was found to be as good as if it had been salted three days, and was as tender as a chicken.

Fresh Produce

Whenever time and conditions permitted, the pioneers broke the thick prairie sod and planted corn, wheat, and vegetables. Often they moved on before the crop matured, leaving the harvest to provide welcome food for those who followed. Later pioneers could expand their menus by using their favorite cellar vegetables, such as onions, carrots, cabbage, turnips, beets, and parsnips.

Fresh vegetables made possible the boiled dinner, a recipe brought from New England. This was a pot of root vegetables, such as potatoes, turnips, onions, and carrots, cooked and flavored with a piece of salt pork or salted beef. If the family ate sparingly, the precious boiled dinner would last for two meals or more and could be eaten the next day with beets added to the original chopped vegetables. This was sometimes called red-flannel hash. Fresh vegetables and produce also added greatly to lentil soups and stews.

Wild and domestic greens made nutritious salads during the trek across the plains and after the pioneers settled in their new homes. Some of the greens picked for salads included watercress, sheep sorrel, jerusalem artichokes, green briar shoots, wild garlic and onions, mustard greens, dandelions, and pig-weed. The greens were washed carefully and sometimes served with an oil and vinegar dressing or with a little salt and sugar. Sometimes a boiled salad dressing was made from cream, vinegar, sugar, and salt.

Breads and Bread Substitutes

Inasmuch as bread was the staff of life, the pioneers struggled with the problems of creating bread or a substitute. Sometimes wheat and potatoes were boiled together and eaten in place of bread because there was no way to grind the wheat. In some places, however, a small coffee grinder was used to grind the grain, and then the wheat was made into mush instead of flour.

Shortly after the coming of the pioneers, flour mills were built and bran, shorts (a kind of cereal), and graham and white flour were produced. The problem of leavening was solved by the use of saleratus, a substance in the soil that was carefully gathered from the

moist ground. Sometimes the saleratus was dried well and used in powdered form such as soda, or it was boiled in a kettle of water and the sediment allowed to settle out. The clear liquid in the kettle was used as a leavening agent.

Sourdough, that mysterious self-replenishing substance, gave the western pioneers their life-sustaining breads and doughs for many arduous months and years. At night, families slept with their sourdough starter to keep the chilly night air from killing the yeast. If a starter died, there would be no biscuits the next day to sop up the beans or stew. Some starters were known to have lasted for years, being used regularly to replenish the family bread supply.

Another popular method of making bread was to use a salt-rising sponge made from warm water, salt, and flour. A pioneer recipe called for one quart water, one teaspoon salt, and flour enough to thicken to a soft dough. These were mixed together and allowed to stand at an even temperature until the mixture became foamy. Since it was difficult to get a good "start" of the sponge, when one was successful the neighbors were called in to share it. To make bread, the sponge was mixed with additional flour and potato water to make a thick dough. It was allowed to rise and then shaped into loaves, put in pans, and allowed to rise again. Then it was ready for baking.

Yeast didn't come into the settlements until later years, when it was brought by Danish immigrants. But before that time, a leavening agent called railroad yeast was sometimes used. It was made by mixing flour, water, salt, shorts, and a little sweetening and ginger, and was kept at an even, warm temperature until it foamed. The railroad yeast was similar to the more familiar sourdough starts that were used in many early-day homes. When yeast did come into use, it was often combined with the salt-rising sponge or the sourdough sponge.

The early settlers who migrated from the Scandinavian countries were skilled in the use of malt. It was made by covering wheat or rye flour with water and letting it stand three or four days until the grain was soft and showed signs of sprouting. Then water was drained off and the sprouts spread out to dry. They were turned often to prevent molding. When dried, the sprouts were browned in the oven, ground, placed in barrels, and covered with water and left to stand until the water showed evidence of "working." The water was drained off for beverages, and the chalky white settlings in the bottom were used to make the yeast as follows: "1 potato boiled and mashed, including the potato water. When luke warm add 1 tablespoon salt, and 2 tablespoons sugar and 1 cup of malt yeast. Stir together and let stand in warm place for about 2 hours, it is then ready for the making of bread." (Kate B. Carter, comp., *Heart Throbs of the West*, Daughters of Utah Pioneers, vol. 1, p. 291.) A cup of yeast was always saved to use in starting the new yeast. The more often the yeast was used, the more successful the bread.

Sugar and Sweetenings

Sugar was a necessary item in the diet that was difficult to obtain in the early years of pioneering. As quickly as possible, gardens were planted, where beets, squash, carrots, and corn were grown. These vegetables are high in sugar content, and the pioneer cook learned to boil them down until a dark, gummy substance was left. This was used for sweetening until honey, molasses, and dried fruit were available.

Honey, provided by swarms of bees brought from the eastern United States, was a necessity as well as a luxury, because it was needed for medicines as well as for sweetening.

Sorghum cane molasses, which was very sweet and had a fine flavor, was second only to flour in importance as a foodstuff. Molasses was on the table for every meal and was also used to sweeten cakes, fruit, and preserves, and to make candy. Early-day homemakers used it to preserve their fruit before they used drying and bottling methods. In fact, molasses was used for all the purposes for which sugar was later used. Beet molasses was as sweet as cane molasses but had a slightly rank flavor, which made it less popular.

Fruit jams and jellies as well as juices were favorites of the thrifty frontier family. As they crossed the plains and traveled through the mountains, the pioneer children and homemakers gathered berries to enhance their meager diets. Their methods of preserving the jams and jellies were simple and adaptable, as we see in this pioneer recipe for elderberry jelly.

Elderberry Jelly

Wash berries and remove pithy stems if desired. Put berries in a large kettle and cover with water. Cook over medium heat for 20 minutes, stirring to prevent sticking. When berries are soft, strain through a clean cloth. Measure juice and add an equal amount of sugar. Bring to boil and stir when necessary. Test for "jellyness" by dropping spoonful into dish. When jelly holds shape, pour into boiled clean jars and seal with wax. (If the fruit didn't jell, the pioneer woman used it as a syrup over buckwheat or johnny cakes.)

Chokecherry jelly is made in a similar fashion, but chokecherries have little or no pectin, so crab apples were added to provide the necessary pectin. The crab apples were washed and cooked for half an hour, then strained. The chokecherries were also washed and cooked until soft, then strained.

The crab apple juice and chokecherry juice were combined, and an equal amount of sugar was added. The juice was then boiled until it clung to a spoon. When the jelling point was reached, the juice was poured into hot sterilized jars and sealed.

Mormon Gravy

The pioneer housewife soon discovered that even sidemeat (bacon) could be used to make a good gravy that added greatly to a meal. The so-called Mormon gravy was made as follows: to 3-4 tablespoons hot fat, left in the pan after frying meat, add 2 tablespoons flour, browning lightly. Remove from fire and add 2 cups liquid, stirring rapidly to prevent lumping. When well blended, return to heat, bring to boil, and add seasonings.

Johnnycakes

2 beaten eggs
2 cups buttermilk
2 tablespoons molasses or honey
2 cups cornmeal
½ cup flour
1 teaspoon soda
1 teaspoon salt
2 tablespoons butter, melted
Beat eggs until light. Add buttermilk and molasses. Sift dry ingredients and add to batter. Add melted butter. Pour into greased pan and bake in hot oven (425° F.) for 20 minutes or until done. Serve by cutting into squares. Makes 24 squares.

Potato Pancakes

4 large potatoes
3 eggs, lightly beaten
Salt and pepper to taste
Peel, wash, and grate potatoes. Add eggs and seasonings. Spoon batter into greased, heated skillet. Brown on each side, turning once. Serves 4.

Lentil Soup

2 cups dried lentils
8 cups water
2 slices bacon, diced
½ cup chopped onion
½ cup chopped celery
¼ cup chopped carrots
3 tablespoons snipped parsley
1 clove garlic, minced
2½ teaspoons salt
¼ teaspoon pepper
2 cups tomatoes
2 tablespoons vinegar
Rinse lentils. Drain. Place in large skillet. Add remaining ingredients except tomatoes and vinegar. Cover and simmer 1½ hours. Add undrained tomatoes and vinegar. Simmer, covered, for 30 minutes. Season to taste. Makes 8-10 servings.

Oxtail Stew

3 lbs. oxtails, cut into 2½-inch pieces
⅓ cup flour
1 teaspoon salt

Pepper
2 tablespoons oil
6 carrots, diced
1 cup chopped onion
1 cup chopped celery
2½ cups meat stock
2 chopped tomatoes
1 bay leaf
¼ teaspoon thyme

Mix flour, salt, and pepper together. Coat oxtails with flour mixture. Brown in hot oil in dutch oven or deep kettle. Remove tails and sauté carrots, onion, and celery in fat until soft but not brown. Add meat stock, tomatoes, bay leaf, and thyme. Bring to boil and add oxtails. Cover and simmer 2½ hours or until tender. Serves 4.

Rusk

Make cornbread and allow to dry for several days; then heat slowly in warmed oven until thoroughly dry and slightly browned. Grate dried bread on a coarse grater or crumble it with a wooden rolling pin. Rusk can be eaten as a cold cereal with cream and sugar or as a tasty, quick mush, with hot milk and honey poured over it.

Homemade Noodles

Combine 1 beaten egg, 2 tablespoons milk, and ½ teaspoon salt. Add enough flour to make stiff dough—about 1 cup. Roll very thin on floured surface and let stand 20 minutes. Roll up loosely and slice ¼-inch wide. Unroll dough. Spread noodles out and let dry for 2 hours, or store in clean cloth bag to keep longer.

Mormon Bread

1 tablespoon dry yeast
1 tablespoon sugar
1 cup potato water
6 cups whole wheat flour
1 rounded tablespoon salt
2 tablespoons honey
2 tablespoons molasses
1 cup lukewarm water
2 rounded tablespoons shortening (bacon drippings, lard, or rendered fat may also be used)

Dissolve yeast in potato water with sugar. Let stand a few minutes. Sift flour and dry ingredients into large bowl. Add yeast mixture, honey, molasses, lukewarm water, and shortening. Stir until easily handled. Form into ball; knead until satiny (15-20 times). Shape into 2 loaves and put into greased bread tins. Let rise one hour, to top of pan. Bake at 350° F. for one hour and 10 minutes. Take from tins and brush tops with butter or shortening. Cool on racks.

Indian Fry Bread

4 cups flour
1 cup dried milk
8 teaspoons baking powder
2 teaspoons salt
2 cups warm water

Mix dry ingredients well; add warm water. Mix and knead until dough is soft but not sticky. Shape into balls 2 inches in diameter; flatten by hand into circles ¼-inch thick. Use flour to keep dough from sticking. (Navajo tradition says one should poke a small hole in the center to release the "evil spirits" before frying.) Fry in hot deep fat. Turn when brown. Tastes good with a little salt or with honey or jam.

Gingersnaps

1 teaspoon ginger
1 tablespoon lard
1 teaspoon soda
1 cup molasses
½ cup water
3 cups flour

Blend together all ingredients except flour. Gradually stir in flour (mixture will be very thick). Knead until dough is soft. Roll thin and cut into 2-inch squares. Place on greased cookie sheet. Sprinkle top with sugar. Bake at 375° F. for 6-7 minutes.

Molasses Candy

1½ cups molasses
¾ cup sugar
1 tablespoon vinegar
1 tablespoon butter
⅛ teaspoon soda
⅛ teaspoon salt

Combine molasses, sugar, and vinegar. Cook to hardball stage. Remove from heat and add butter, soda, and salt. Stir until soda is blended, then pour into greased pan. When cool, pull between greased fingertips until white and stiff. Form into ropes; place on buttered plate until cool, then cut into pieces.

Honey Candy

2 cups honey
1 cup sugar
1 cup cream

Combine ingredients and cook slowly until hardball stage. Pour into buttered tin and when cool enough to handle, butter hands and pull to a light golden color. Break into pieces when cool.

SOURDOUGH RECIPES

Sourdough Starter

Sourdough is almost as popular today as it was in pioneer times. The starter, made from a culture of flour, water, and yeast, is generally made in a crock or heavy glass container. It can be made by mixing 1 cup flour, ½ yeast cake or ½ package dry yeast and 1 teaspoon sugar. Add about 1½ cups warm water and mix into a thick batter. Allow to rise and become bubbly overnight, then add 1 cup flour and warm water to make a thick batter; repeat for two or three days, then allow to set for one to three days until the batter becomes active.

Each time some of the starter is used, equal parts of flour and water or warm milk are added (for example, if ½ cup starter has been used, then ½ cup warm water and ½ cup flour are blended into the remaining starter); then the mixture is covered and left to stand in a warm place several hours or overnight until bubbles reappear. Cover the container and store the starter in a cool place until needed. (It keeps best when it is used regularly.) In pioneer times neighbors often shared their starter, and an original starter sometimes lasted for many months.

Sourdough Bread

2 cups warm water
1 cup sourdough starter
6-8 cups flour, unsifted
2 teaspoons sugar
2 teaspoons salt

In large bowl combine the water, starter, and 2 cups flour. Cover and let stand 8 hours or overnight (until sponge is bubbly and spongy looking). Stir into sponge the salt, sugar, and enough flour to make stiff dough. Put on floured board and knead dough until satiny, adding flour as necessary. Shape into oblong or round loaves and place on lightly greased baking sheet. Cover and let rise. Brush with water. Score top of loaf with sharp knife. Bake at 400° F. until crust is browned—about 30-35 minutes. Cool on racks. Yields 2 loaves.

Sourdough Pancakes

1 cup sourdough starter
1 cup flour
1 cup water
2 eggs
6 tablespoons oil
1 tablespoon sugar
1 teaspoon salt
1 teaspoon baking powder
½ teaspoon salt
Milk

Combine sourdough starter, flour, and water.

Let mixture stand overnight. Then add remaining ingredients and enough milk to make a smooth batter. Fry on hot griddle.

Buckwheat Griddle Cakes

3 cups buckwheat flour
1 cup white flour
1 teaspoon salt
1 tablespoon dry yeast
¼ cup warm water
1 teaspoon granulated sugar
3¾ cups lukewarm water
2 tablespoons brown sugar
¾ teaspoon baking soda
1 tablespoon cooking oil

Sift both flours and salt together. Soften yeast in ¼ cup warm water. Dissolve sugar in 3¾ cups lukewarm water. Add yeast to sugar-water mixture, and stir into dry ingredients. Mix well. Cover and let stand overnight at room temperature. In the morning, stir batter. Add brown sugar, soda, and oil. (Refrigerate 1 cup batter for starter. It will keep for several weeks.) Spoon out on hot lightly greased griddle, and turn when bubbly. Serve with warm molasses or maple syrup. Makes 20 pancakes.

To re-use starter, add 1 cup lukewarm water, ½ cup buckwheat flour, and ½ cup white flour to 1 cup starter. Stir until smooth. Let stand overnight as before. When ready to bake, add 2 tablespoons brown sugar, 1 tablespoon cooking oil, ½ teaspoon salt, and ½ teaspoon soda. Reserve 1 cup batter for starter again.

CHAPTER TWO

PRESERVING AND DRYING FOODS

The great outdoors provided the pioneer woman's culinary treasure trove. She gathered fragrant herbs—basil, ginger, mint, sage, and parsley—and used them to enhance her cooking. She preserved apples, berries, and other fruits to make fruit butter, cider, and jams.

Preserving foods by drying them is perhaps the oldest preservation method used by man. The Indians knew about the process and used it for centuries, and many of the pioneers had used the method in their homes in the East. In colonial times, settlers had preserved apples, beans, corn, and peppers by sun-drying them, stringing them on linen thread, and hanging them across the chimneys of their fireplaces or among the rafters, where they provided decoration as well as the winter food supply.

Drying was the best way known at that time to preserve and store the fruits of summer against the austerity of the winter. The dried foods were a boon to the restricted diets of the early settlers. Because a large percentage of the water was removed, the nutrients—vitamins, sugar, and minerals—were in a concentrated form, and the sweet dried fruits were a favorite confection. They were also used in many recipes, either chopped, ground, or added whole. One favorite recipe was this one:

Pioneer Fruit Candy

1 pound raisins
½ pound figs

½ pound dates
1 cup prunes, pitted
Juice and rind of 1 orange
1 cup chopped nuts

Grind fruits and orange rind. Blend with juice and nuts. Shape into balls or bars. Let stand overnight to blend flavors and ripen. The candies can be dipped in melted chocolate or rolled in coconut for added variety.

An early pioneer diary recalls the festivity associated with the fruit-drying process:

An evening social, which we called a "peach cutting," was looked forward to with happy anticipation. We worked like Trojans all day gathering fifteen or more bushels of peaches which were to be cut that evening by our invited guests. These were put out to dry on a scaffold and housetops the next day. Besides gathering the peaches, we made several pumpkin pies and doughnuts for refreshments and stacked up brush and dried weeds

for a huge bonfire. Around the fire we played "Run Sheep Run" and other games. So, with all the hard work, there were times of real enjoyment, which we created from our own environment. (Tanner, A Mormon Mother, p. 40.)

The process of drying was simple, the results mouth-watering. The procedures followed by the pioneer housewife were almost identical to those used today. Fruit selected for drying must be sound, fresh, and at the right stage of maturity—neither underripe nor overripe. Bruised or overripe fruit was discarded because it easily blemished and was prone to spoil; underripe fruit had little flavor after dehydration and was less colorful. After selection, the fruit was washed and then prepared according to the type used. For apricots, the pits were removed and the fruit cut in halves. Peaches were pitted, peeled, and sliced. Plums were sliced or pitted and halved.

Some fruits changed color and flavor during drying. To prevent this, the fruit was sometimes steamed or scalded to preserve the color: It was placed in a cheesecloth bag and steamed over boiling water in a closed container, or it was plunged into boiling water for four to five minutes. It was then drained well and dried with a towel and spread out to dry in the sun. The fruit was brought in at night to keep out dew and humidity and was taken back out into the warmth of the sun again the next morning. It was left in the sun to dry for several days, depending on the fruit and the heat of the sun.

Sometimes the fruit was spread to dry on handwoven mats that were made by Indians and early pioneers, who gathered willow reeds, stripped the bark from them, then dried and wove them into loose-meshed surfaces. These mats were clean and kept the fruit protected from dirt and dust. Later, wooden frames were made to hold the foods during the drying time. Dried foods were stored in clean cloth bags in a dry, cool, dark place.

Western pioneers were often blessed with an abundance of corn, a plant that was long familiar to the Indians. The most successful method of preserving the surplus corn was to dry the kernels in the summer sun for use in the winter months.

To sun-dry corn, settlers removed the husks and silk from the ears, which were then dropped into a large pot of boiling salted water. When the water returned to the boiling point, the corn was cooked just a few minutes to "set the milk." The corn was then removed from the kettle and cooled, and the kernels cut from the cob.

The cut corn was spread in shallow pans and covered with a layer of cheesecloth. The pan was then set in direct sunlight until the kernels were thoroughly dry to the touch, which took about 6 to 8 hours in the hot sun. If the corn didn't dry the first day, the pans were brought indoors overnight and set out the next morning to finish the process. The dried kernels kept well in clean covered bags or jars at room temperature.

To prepare the dried corn, the kernels were washed clean in hot water and covered

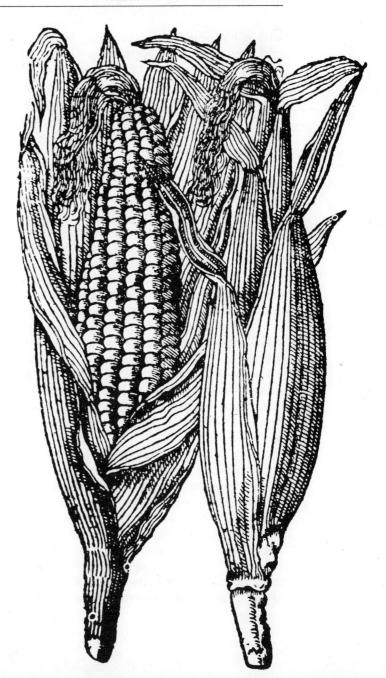

with a hot liquid, such as water, broth, or milk, and allowed to soak for at least six hours or overnight. To cook, the corn was heated without draining and allowed to simmer, covered, until tender, about 45 minutes. Water was added as necessary. The corn was then drained and seasoned with butter, salt, and pepper to taste.

For today's homemaker, drying of fruits and vegetables is also practical. The method used remains much the same as that used by the pioneer women with a few exceptions. One exception is the use of a process called sulfuring, which preserves color in dried fruit, avoids browning, and decreases the loss of vitamins A and C in the fruit. Sulfuring can be accomplished in two ways, one used indoors and the other outdoors.

The indoor process is called sodium dip, which is prepared by dissolving 1 tablespoon sodium bisulfite in 1 gallon water. The prepared fruit is dipped into the solution and soaked for ten minutes before drying. *Sodium bisulfite* or *sodium sulfite* can be purchased from a druggist and should not be confused with *sodium bisulfate*.

The outdoor process is accomplished by burning sulfur fumes in an enclosed container to preserve the fruit. This process calls for slotted wooden trays on which to set the fruit and a tightly constructed wooden box to go over the trays. If more than one tray is used in the box, the trays should be at least 1 inch apart to let the sulfur fumes circulate freely. A small opening is cut in the bottom of the box to light the sulfur and provide ventilation.

The sulfur is placed in a shallow clean tin can, using 2 teaspoons of sulfur for each pound of fruit. The can is then set beside the trays and lighted with a match. The sulfur fumes are allowed to burn and circulate for the alloted time for the particular fruit being dried. The fruit is prepared for sulphuring as for sun drying. After the fruit has been sulfured, it may be dried by the sun or in the oven.

Before fruits or vegetables are dried in

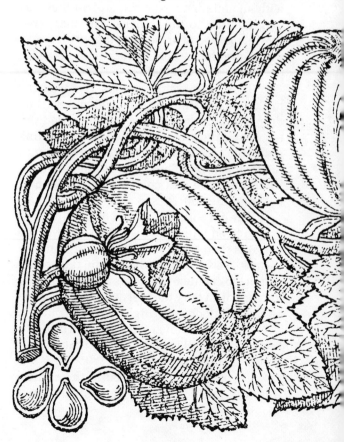

the sun, they may be steamed or blanched for a short time to "set" the color and flavor. Steaming is done by using a large kettle with a tight-fitting lid. The fruits or vegetables are placed in a wire basket or steamer above the boiling water in the kettle. The produce should not be more than 2½ inches thick, and should never touch the water. Each piece of fruit or vegetable should be heated through until tender but not completely cooked. The produce to be dried is then spread in a thick

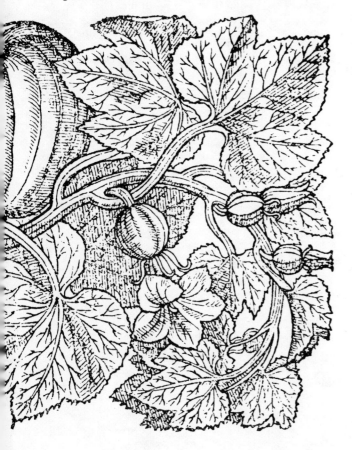

layer on drying trays and placed in direct sunlight. Fruits are placed skin-side down to prevent juices from dripping out. Vegetables should not be exposed in the sun for more than a day or two or they may become scorched. Drying can be completed in the shade if necessary.

Oven drying can be efficient and convenient if the weather outdoors is not conducive to sun drying. The trays used in the oven should be slightly smaller than the oven racks, to provide good heat circulation. Do not dry more than four to six pounds of food at a time. Two to four trays may be used at a time; place them at least 2½ inches apart and allow 3 to 4 inches of space at top and bottom of the oven. Set the oven heat at 150° F. Set the trays of fruit in the oven and leave the oven door ajar at least 8 inches if a gas oven is used, less if the oven is electric. This helps control the heat and lets out the moist air. The fruit should be turned and rotated frequently during the drying to prevent scorching, and the room should be well ventilated during the drying time.

Dried fruit and vegetables should be stored in air-tight containers at cool temperatures and out of direct light. Glass, plastic, or tin containers with tight-fitting lids may be used. High temperatures, light, and air speed the deterioration and discoloration of the foods and make them less appetizing. Dried foods should not be kept for more than a year.

A table of methods of preparation and times involved in drying fruits and vegetables follows.

**SIMPLIFIED
DIRECTIONS
FOR PREPARING
AND DRYING
FRUITS AND
VEGETABLES**

VEGETABLES	SELECTION AND PREPARATION	TREATMENT BEFORE DRYING	TIME IN MINUTES	TESTS FOR DRYNESS
Beans; bush varieties	Remove defective pods. Wash. Remove Strings from string varieties. Split pods lengthwise to hasten drying.	Steam or pressure saucepan	15 to 20 (steam) 5 (pressure cook)	Brittle
Beets	Select small tender beets of good color and flavor. Wash; trim the tops but leave the crowns. Steam for 30 to 45 minutes, until cooked through. Cool; trim off the roots and crowns; peel. Cut into shoestring strips or into slices about ⅛" thick.	Steam	30 to 45	Tough; leathery
Broccoli	Trim and cut as for serving. Wash. Quarter stalks lengthwise.	Steam	8 to 10	Brittle
Cabbage	Remove outer leaves, quarter, and core. Cut into shreds about ⅛" thick.	Steam	5 to 6 (until wilted)	Tough to brittle
Carrots	Select crisp, tender carrots. Wash; trim off the roots and tops. Cut into slices or strips about ⅛" thick.	Steam	8 to 10	Tough; leathery
Corn (cut)	Select tender, sweet corn. Husk; steam on the cob immediately, 10 or 15 minutes, or until milk is set. Cut corn from cob.	Steam	30	Dry; brittle
Celery, parsley, mint	Select young, tender leaves. Remove stems.	Wash	0	Brittle
Onions	Remove outer, discolored layers. Slice.	None	0	Brittle; light colored
Peas	Select young, tender peas of a sweet variety. Shell.	Steam immediately	10	Hard, wrinkled
Potatoes	Peel, cut into shoestring strips 3/16" in cross section, or cut into slices about ⅛" thick.	Rinse in cold water; steam	4 to 6	Brittle
Spinach, chard, beet greens	Select young, tender leaves. Wash. See that leaves are not wadded when placed on trays. Cut crosswise into several pieces to facilitate drying.	Steam	4, or until thoroughly wilted	Brittle
Squash (banana)	Wash, peel, and slice in strips ¼" thick	Steam	6	Tough to brittle
Squash (Hubbard) Pumpkin	Chop into strips about 1 inch wide. Peel off rind. Scrape off the fiber and seeds. Cut peeled strips crosswise into pieces about ¼" thick.	Steam	Until tender	Tough
Squash (summer) crookneck, scallop, zucchini, etc.	Wash, trim, and cut into ¼" slices.	Steam	6	Brittle

VEGETABLES	SELECTION AND PREPARATION	TREATMENT BEFORE DRYING	TIME IN MINUTES	TESTS FOR DRYNESS
Tomatoes for stewing	Select tomatoes of good color. Steam or dip in boiling water to loosen skins. Chill in cold water. Peel. Cut tomato into sections, not over ¾'' wide.	No further treatment is necessary	10 to 20	Leathery
Powdered vegetables	For use in soup or puree, powder leafy vegetables after drying by grinding fine in a blender or Osterizer.			
Soup mixture	Cut vegetables into small pieces; prepare and dry according to directions for each vegetable. Combine and store. Satisfactory combinations may be made from cabbage, carrots, celery, corn, onions, and peas. Rice, dry beans, or split peas, and meat stock are usually added at the time of cooking.			

FRUITS	SELECTION AND PREPARATION	TREATMENT BEFORE DRYING	TIME IN MINUTES	TESTS FOR DRYNESS
Apples	Peel and core. Cut into slices or rings about ⅛'' thick.	Sulfur	60	Leathery; glove-like section cut in half, no moist areas.
Berries (except strawberries)	Pick over; wash if necessary.	Steam	½ to 1	Hard; no visible moisture when crushed
Cherries	Pit only large cherries.	White cherries may be sulfured	10 to 15	Leathery but sticky
Figs	If figs are small or have partly dried on the tree, they may be dried whole without blanching. Otherwise, cut in half.	Steam	20	Pliable; leathery; slightly sticky
Grapes Small plums and prunes	If dried without blanching, a much longer drying time is required. Only Thompson seedless or other seedless varieties should be dried.	Blanching or no treatment		Pliable; leathery
Pears	Peel, cut in half lengthwise, and core. Section or cut into slices about 1'' thick.	Sulfur	60 if sliced 120 if quartered	Springy texture
Large-stone fruits (peaches, apricots, nectarines, large plums and prunes, etc.)	Peel and slice peaches. Cut in half and pit apricots, nectarines, and large plums and prunes. Fruits dry more rapidly if cut in quarters or sliced.	Steam (may omit) and sulfur	60 if sliced 120 if quartered	Pliable; leathery; a handful of prunes properly dried will fall apart after squeezing

CHAPTER THREE

HOMEMADE REMEDIES

When sickness struck the family, the pioneer woman called upon every resource at her command to alleviate the illness and save the lives of her loved ones. Since many of the early homesteads were isolated and no help was available, it fell upon the mother to provide the necessary, often meager, medical care for her family. Sometimes her efforts were successful. Sometimes, due to the dearth of adequate and accurate medical knowledge in the frontier, they were not.

Always resourceful in times of need, the frontier woman learned by trial and error which seeds, roots, weeds, and blossoms of the prairie plants would be efficacious in times of sickness. Many of these pioneer remedies had a sound basis in medicine and are still effective. Other treatments have long since fallen into the realm of superstition and folklore.

Along with her homespun remedies, the mother in those early days exercised her faith in healing by the Spirit, through administrations of the priesthood; and along with her measure of medicine, she administered strong doses of prayers and faith. Many pioneer diaries and journals, as well as medical records, testify to the effectiveness of both the prayers and the potions used in the homes.

Among the favorite remedies were herb teas, concoctions that had medicinal properties attributed to them through centuries of cultivation and use. The pioneers often found these teas, brewed from familiar growing plants, efficacious and refreshing.

Such herb teas were thought to have properties that "causeth the mind and heart to become merry and reviveth the heart of faintings and swooning and drives away troubles and thoughts out of the mind arising from melancholy or black choler." ("Herb Teas to Enjoy This Winter," *Glamour*, October 1973, p. 74.)

The same writer urges a tisane of sweet marjoram to quiet the "wamblings of the stomacke" at sea; a cup of "breathful camomile to soothe the aching of a man's head"; a refreshing infusion of balm to "renew youth, strengthen the brain, relieve languishing nature and prevent baldness" at one and the same time! (Ibid.) These are but a few of the herb teas and concoctions, fragrant

with flavor and history, that provided for the pioneers the pleasantest and simplest relief for minor pains and discomforts, as well as some more serious ailments. Although herbal teas and home-brewed medicines are somewhat of an anachronism in a world increasingly dependent on pills, many of the old, highly esteemed, infusions have survived and are used today, because they are pleasant to drink; and quite a few are healthful beverages with soothing properties.

COMMON PIONEER HERBS AND THEIR USES

Medicinal and Herb Teas

Nature was lavish with herbs for tea. Pioneer women carefully picked leaves and roots to make flavorful teas to warm or cure their families. A cup of hot mint or sage tea brewed in a treasured earthenware pot was refreshing to the pioneer woman seeking a gracious home life for her family. Dropping the dried leaves into boiling water and letting them steep linked her with generations of women who had used this familiar ritual of hospitality and well-being through the ages.

The method of making the drinks remains the same today. Bring the water to a boil, then remove it from the heat, and add the leaves. Usually one teaspoonful of leaves is used with each cup of water. Cover the pot and let it stand for three to five minutes. The water should not be boiled after the leaves are added, and the pot should be covered during the steeping time.

Common pioneer teas and their properties are listed below:

ALFALFA A tea made from the leaves of alfalfa, which was thought to cure arthritis and to be a good remedy for rheumatism.

ANGELICA A balm of angelica, lemon peel, and nutmeg, used to treat nervous headaches and neuralgia and whenever a tonic or stimulant was needed. It was believed to have great restorative properties.

ANISE Anise leaves, thought to be beneficial for bronchitis, asthma, and nausea. In ancient times the Romans made cakes with it, to be served after rich meals to counteract indigestion.

BLUE VIOLET The leaves, roots, and flowers of this plant were thought to be good for purifying blood. The tea was used to relieve severe headaches, coughs, and whooping cough, and to dissolve mucus. A gargle made from the tea was used for swollen throats.

BRIGHAM TEA Made from mountain rush, this popular tea, sometimes called "Squaw Tea," was widely used for medicinal purposes. Today this herb has been analyzed in the laboratory and found to have organic copper in its stems, an element considered to be a very good germ killer. The pioneers learned about the plant from the Indians, who had used it for centuries as a medicine."

BURDOCK A tea made from the root of this common plant was believed to be an excellent blood purifier as well as cure for gout, rheumatism, canker sores, skin diseases, boils, and carbuncles. A hot fomentation of the tea was considered good for swelling.

CAMOMILE This anciently known plant provided leaves that acted as a sedative and as a cure for indigestion. It was taken before bedtime to relax the patient.

CATNIP This tea was used for colic and gas, especially for infants and children. A little honey was often added to make it more palatable. It was also used for fevers, headaches, and expelling worms. An enema made from the tea was used for children in convulsions.

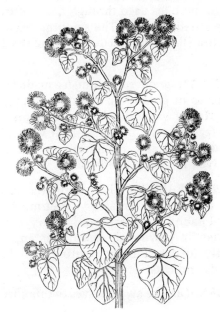

CHERRY The green bark of the wild cherry, cut when the sap was up, was boiled to make a tea believed to help build up the blood. Cherry bark was also used as a cough syrup, made by boiling a cup of cherry bark in a pint of water and adding honey. It was cooked until thick and syrupy, then used for colds and rheumatism.

COMFREY The root and leaves of this plant were used as a remedy for lung problems, coughs, colds, hemorrhage, asthma, and tuberculosis, and were sometimes used in treating ulceration of the kidneys, stomach, or bowels. Poultices of leaves were used for bruises, sprains, swellings, fractures, broken bones, and ulcers.

DILL An herb tea used through the centuries for its sedative effect. The soothing brew is made from the seeds, not the leaves, of the dill plant.

GINGER A fragrant, refreshing tea made from the leaves or ground-up roots of the ginger plant. Honey was added for increased medicinal effectiveness. Ginger tea, made with milk and sugar, was also a comforting drink that was given to young children.

GOLDEN SEAL This bitter herb was made into a tea for treating rheumatism, stomachache, cankers, and many other illnesses. In powdered form it was applied directly to the skin for treating puncture wounds and cuts.

GOLDENROD The sweet leaves of this shrub, when crushed, had an aroma of anise. Goldenrod grew on dry hillsides and was a familiar plant to the pioneers, who used it for a variety of aches and pains.

HOPS This plant was used to induce sleep when necessary. It was also used as a remedy for toothache, earache, and neuralgia, and was thought to be a liver tonic. It was also used in treating diseases of the chest and throat.

HOREHOUND This bitter herb, used in teas for a variety of ailments, was also used to make a candy that was a favorite of pioneer children.

LADYSLIPPER The leaves of the ladyslipper were dried and ground to a powder, then added to hot water to make a tea to stimulate and build up the blood.

MARSHMALLOW A tea used in treating lung troubles, hoarseness, dysentery, diarrhea, catarrh, pneumonia, and kidney diseases, it was also used to bathe sore and inflamed eyes. It has a high vitamin A content, and as a poultice it was considered useful in relieving sore and inflamed parts.

MINT Tea made from the dried leaves of peppermint was used against heat prostration and nausea and was considered good for stomach troubles. Sometimes the dried rinds of oranges or lemons were added to a quart of dried mint leaves, a teaspoon of ground cloves, and a cup of marigold petals to make a mint-flavored tea. The mixture was stored in a dry, airtight container until needed.

MULLEIN A tea of mullein leaves was used for asthma, croup, bronchitis, lung infections, hay fever, bleeding from the lungs, as a throat gargle, for toothache, and for washing open sores. It was believed to induce sleep and relieve pain. Warm fomentations were used for glandular swellings, such as mumps. With a spoonful of sugar or syrup, the tea was used as a cough suppressant.

PARSLEY A remedy for jaundice and other liver ailments, fevers, kidney ailments, and gallstones.

PENNYROYAL Used as a medicinal tea, these leaves were rubbed on the face and arms for a mosquito repellent.

PEPPERS Hot, red peppers, found in an abundance in the Southwest, were left by the fire to dry, then pounded, steeped for tea, and drunk to cure colds.

PINE NEEDLES These were sometimes boiled to make a tea for use in treating colds.

RED RASPBERRY LEAF Used to treat flu and colds, dysentery, and diarrhea in children.

SAGE A long-time favorite of the ancients as well as pioneers, sage was used to treat ailments of the liver, blood, brain, and eyes. It was believed to aid in a long and healthy life.

SASSAFRAS Dried and powdered to make tea, the roots of this plant were used to build blood and treat blood disorders.

SPEARMINT Spearmint tea was prescribed for colic, stomach gas, dyspepsia, spasms, dropsy, nausea and vomiting (especially in pregnancy), bladder and kidney stones, and inflammation. It was believed to be soothing and quieting to the nerves, and helpful for diarrhea and nervous headaches. Its tangy mint flavor made it a long-time favorite of the pioneers.

STRAWBERRY LEAVES Made into a tea, this was considered helpful in treating diarrhea.

SUNFLOWER The seeds and the leaves of this wild flower were made into a tea for treating diarrhea.

WINTERGREEN This fern was made into a fragrant tea that was believed helpful in curing colds.

WILLOW LEAVES Believed to be beneficial for treating diarrhea and to relieve the pain and itching caused by poison ivy.

YARROW A remedy used to treat fevers, including typhoid fever; hemorrhage, hemorrhoids, diarrhea, diabetes, stomach gas, measles, chicken pox, and smallpox.

YELLOW DOCK Used to treat impure blood, fungus, glandular tumors, swellings, ulcerated eyelids, and itch.

OTHER PIONEER TREATMENTS

The pioneers had many favorite treatments for their physical ailments. Most of these were palliative measures, but some of them were remedial. A list of some of the more common treatments follows.

ACHES Toothache, earache, and headache were treated in a variety of ways. One method used heat applied to the afflicted part, to relieve the pain. Hot ashes were put in a cloth, dampened, and held over the sore tooth or ear. Earaches were also treated with a brew of hops and by applying fomentations of hot yellow dock tea. Hops and mullein were used to treat toothache, while mustard leaves, angelica, spearmint, catnip, and blue violet teas were used to treat headaches.

BLEEDING Bleeding was stopped by applying a poultice of turpentine and brown sugar to the wound. Lampblack was sometimes applied directly to the wound or mixed with lard to make a poultice. Pine resin was another remedy used for bleeding. Comfrey, mullein, and yarrow were used to stem hemorrhages.

BLOOD BUILDERS Greens such as dandelion leaves, nasturtium leaves, leaves of the poke plant, and other plants were washed, boiled, and seasoned, then eaten as "messes." These early salads were considered healthful and efficacious in restoring tired and sick bodies.

BROKEN BONES These were set and splinted by using sticks or boards, or with hard abode clay, applied while damp and then dried to form a solid cast.

BURNS Many homemade remedies were used to "draw out" the fire. Some were helpful; others only aggravated the burn. Poultices applied to the burn were made from such materials as potatoes and linseed oil, lard and flour, mutton grease, castor oil and egg white, chestnut leaves, and table salt dissolved in warm water.

CHEST CONGESTION Poultices of various kinds were used as counter-irritants to relieve croup and congestion in the lungs. Usually these mixtures caused reddening of the skin and needed to be watched closely to prevent burning. The chest would be protected by applying oil or a thin layer of cloth directly to the skin before putting on the poultice. Some favorite mixtures included kerosene, turpentine, and lard; dry mustard and flour mixed with water to form a paste; hot mutton tallow mixed with camphor or lard; pine tar and turpentine; onion poultice made by soaking rags in onion juice; groundhog or goose oil rubbed on the chest and covered with a hot flannel cloth.

COLDS Pine needles were sometimes boiled to make a strong tea to treat colds. Powdered quince was another remedy. The recipe called for "enough powdered quince to lay on the blade of a knife, added to hot water." One pioneer journal recommended drinking the brine from pickled sauerkraut; this made the patient thirsty enough to drink lots of water, which helped cure the cold. Also recommended for colds were wintergreen, rosemary, hot peppers, raspberry leaf, and mullein.

One treatment for colds was homemade nosedrops made by combining 1 cup water, ¼ teaspoon salt, and ½ teaspoon baking soda. This was boiled 2-3 minutes, then cooled and poured into an empty sterile bottle.

CHAPPED HANDS Hands were softened by rubbing pine resin or mutton tallow on them. Pioneer women who washed or sorted wool also found that the lanolin in the wool helped soften their skin.

COLIC This was treated by massaging the stomach lightly with warm towels or warm castor oil. Another remedy was to administer a potion consisting of a pinch of soda in a spoonful of water. Ginseng root was believed helpful and could be taken by chewing the roots or by boiling them in a pint of water and then straining and drinking them.

A favorite cure for colic was the use of asafetida. Falling into the realm of folk-lore medicine, the practice of putting asafetida in a bag and tying it around the baby's neck for six months was believed to keep colic away. Asafetida tied around the neck was also believed to be a preventive measure against contagious diseases, and during times of contagion a number of children wore the smelly bags. Some people wore the bags all year, every year, regardless of the season or the state of their health.

CROUPS AND COUGHS Coughs were cured by a variety of herbs and homemade medicines, including cherry bark syrup, a mixture of honey and vinegar, the juice of an onion, mutton tallow and beeswax rubbed on the back and chest, and a drop of turpentine in a spoonful of sugar. A poultice made from lard, turpentine, and kerosene was sometimes put on a flannel cloth and then placed over the chest and neck.

A pioneer medicine for treating whooping cough was made with ½ cup brown sugar, the juice of 3 lemons, 2 egg whites, and a bottle of olive oil. This mixture was given a teaspoon at a time to the sick child.

A cough syrup recipe for less serious illness involved combining ⅓ cup brown sugar and ¼ cup honey in a large glass. Into this was stirred about a cup of water in which 8-10 whole cloves had been boiled. (The cloves were strained out.)

DIARRHEA Herbs used to treat diarrhea included sunflower leaves made into a tea and used sparingly (it was considered very potent), strawberry leaves, red raspberry leaves, marshmallow, spearmint, willow leaves, and yarrow.

FEVER Catnip was used for reducing fevers, as was parsley taken in a drink two or three times a day. Yarrow was used for all kinds of fevers, including typhoid fever.

HAIR PROBLEMS Camomile tea was used as a rinse to keep blond hair from darkening, and yarrow was believed to help prevent balding.

HEART TROUBLE Favorite herbs for heart trouble included pungent garlic, which was eaten either raw or cooked, and sassafras tea.

HEMORRHOIDS Piles were treated by using warm enemas made from spearmint tea, yarrow, and catnip.

ITCH A standard treatment for the itch, a highly contagious ailment caused by a small parasite, was sulfur and lard mixed together and applied to the skin. Another home remedy was sulfur burned in a metal container in a closed area, with the patient breathing the pungent fumes. Herbs used to relieve itching included willow leaves, poultices of burdock or yellow dock, and mustard leaves.

INSECT BITES Bee stings and other insect bites were treated with mud, clay mixed with water, turpentine, kerosene, crushed chrysanthemum leaves, butter and salt mixtures, ragweed that was crushed or mashed and applied to the skin, linseed oil, oatmeal water, buttermilk, a mixture of epsom salts and baking soda, or a mixture of witch hazel and boric acid. These were all applied to the affected part of the skin and were supposed to relieve the pain and itching.

INDIGESTION There were many treatments for stomach disorders, including the tea of wild peppermint, spearmint, catnip with honey, and ginger, anise, and camomile teas. A home medicine for pain in the intestinal track was made by simmering one cup rice (without salt or sugar) in 3-4 cups water for eight to ten minutes until it became milky. The rice water was then taken by the patient while it was still hot.

KIDNEY and LIVER AILMENTS Kidney ailments were treated with spearmint, marshmallow, and comfrey herbs. Liver function was believed to be helped by the use of sage, parsley, and hops.

NAUSEA Anise was thought to be useful for nausea, as were mint and spearmint teas.

RHEUMATISM Alfalfa tea was sometimes used for rheumatism, as were angelica, cherry bark, burdock, and golden seal.

RINGWORM One treatment for ringworm was a poultice made from walnut shells. The green walnut shells were cracked open, crushed, and applied to the affected areas.

SEDATIVES To relax the patient before bedtime, teas made from camomile, dill, hops, ginger, spearmint, catnip, or mullein were administered.

TONICS A spring tonic for a gentle purging of the system was believed to be helpful to pioneer well-being. A great many herbs were used for this yearly ritual, including hops, yellow dock, sage, golden seal, ladyslipper, burdock, sassafras, ginger, angelica, and rhubarb.

TONSILLITIS A pioneer medicine for treating tonsillitis consisted of a homemade salve made by heating 2 tablespoons mutton tallow in a frying pan with six balm of gilead buds. As the buds cooked, they were mashed up. Then the mixture was strained and cooled. If put in a covered jar, the salve could be kept for years. It was used to treat erysipelas and other skin infections and was also used as an ointment to be rubbed on the chest to treat tonsillitis.

TEMPERAMENT In an early pioneer newspaper was this humorous recipe intended to cure ills of temperament.

A complete cure for a terrible disorder of the mouth, commonly called "Scandal": Take a good nature, one ounce, of an herb called by the Mormons "mind your own business," one ounce, to which add of the oil of benevolence, one drachim and of brotherly love, two ounces. You must mix the preceding ingredients with a little charity for others, and a few sprigs of "keep your tongue between your teeth." Let this compound be allowed to simmer for a short time in a vessel called circumspection and it will be ready for use.

Symptoms: The symptoms are violent itching in the tongue and roof of the mouth when you are in company with a species of animal called "Gossips."

Applications: When you feel a fit of the disorder coming on, take a teaspoonful of the mixture, hold it in your mouth, which you must keep closely shut till you get home. (Mary K. Stout, "From a Nauvoo Pantry," *New Era*, December 1973, p. 44.)

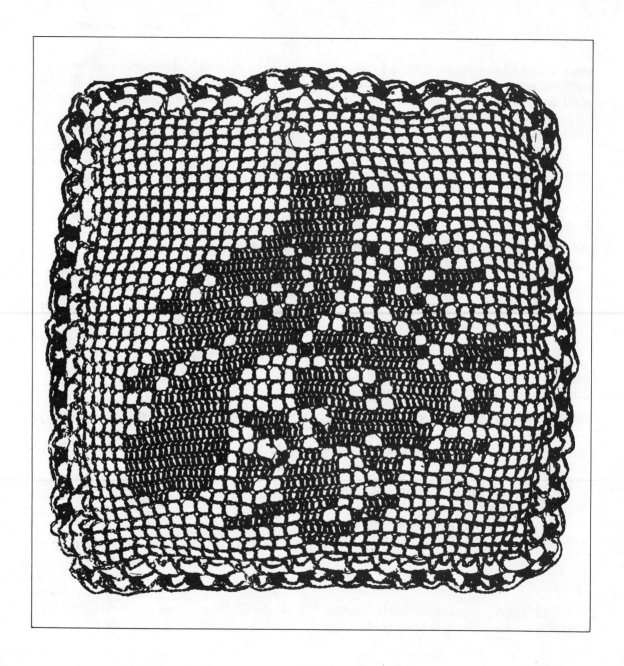

CHAPTER FOUR

NEEDLE ARTS

The pioneer women who came to the West from England, Ireland, France, Denmark, Norway, the Netherlands, and other countries brought with them only the small number of possessions they could fit into the tight quarters of a covered wagon. A few precious needles brought across the ocean from the old country might have lasted a lifetime, and every scrap of linen and homespun was considered valuable. Nothing was thrown away.

Though limited in material possessions, the pioneers brought a wealth of knowledge based on their cherished old-world traditions of homemaking skills and crafts. A journal records the skill of one of those early women:

Mother was an accomplished artist at needle work. Her industry in this line, as she plied her needle when crossing the ocean in a sailboat, attracted the attention of the captain and his wife for whom my mother sewed, and thus she enjoyed the best accommodations on board. When she was traveling across the plains to Salt Lake Valley, she made yards of fine muslin embroidery with which she trimmed her first baby clothes. I noticed a small mark of yellow on the embroidery and asked her what it was.

"That mark," she said, "is a little iron rust from a wire on the bow of the wagon where I tied my work when crossing the plains." The fact that all her children were blessed [christened] in those same clothes illustrates the care she gave to things of value. (Tanner, *A Mormon Mother*, pp. 3-4.)

When pioneer families reached their destination in the rugged western country, they soon learned that materials for embellishing their modest frontier homes were not readily available. Imported yarns and fabrics were too expensive and scarce. So, undaunted, most women began to make their own. From sheep fleece they carded, spun, dyed, and wove their own wool yarn. They began raising flax to produce linen thread. Their desire for lovely things even motivated an adventure in sericulture, the raising of silkworms.

They learned new needlework skills from friendly Indians who had developed elaborate techniques of needlework using quills of porcupines and birds to create patterns on soft doeskin jackets, moccasins, and shirts. From the Indians they also learned to experiment with dyes, brewing rich brown from the black walnut husks, purple from pokeberries, clear yellow from goldenrod, and blue from the indigo plant.

It is interesting to visualize these long-ago women in their crude cabins in the frontier settlements serenely plying their needles while danger and hardships, sickness and hunger were ever-present threats. Yet these intrepid women were not satisfied to make clothing, bedding, and table linens that were merely functional. They longed for self-expression and were able to find it in their needlework.

Lacking patterns, they drew upon their imaginations and European backgrounds, sometimes sharing a motif with a neighbor.

Even when often-used patterns were copied, the result was individual, for the work was done by human hands and not by machine. In their inspired needlework they sometimes captured the quick scarlet flash of a bird, the graceful leap of a deer, the solidarity of a log cabin, the serenity of a sheaf of wheat, the warmth of a sunrise over the desert. Other themes were taken from Bible stories or quotations, from patriotic emblems, and from familiar objects in nature, including flowers, trees, birds, and bees. For the Mormon pioneers the beehive was a much loved symbol, as were the likenesses of the Church presidents and other leaders.

Knitting, crocheting, tatting, needle-point, hardanger, and embroidery were all handwork skills that proved useful and practical in helping the frontier housewife create a home in a new land. Clothing and household linens were frequently embellished with the exquisite handwork of the skilled seamstress. Sheets, pillowcases, pillow shams, table covers, towels, napkins, blankets, petticoats, dresses, hats, scarves, quilts, baby clothes, shawls, Bible covers, pin cushions, suspenders, watch holders, purses and bags, chair seats, diaper bags, bell pulls, samplers, nightgowns, and caps—all were created or embellished with needlework.

Of all these needle arts, perhaps the sampler is the most typical and characteristic of the times. It was small enough for a child to hold comfortably, to work on or to tuck away in a pocket. Little girls were taught to "sew a fine seam" by their mothers and grandmothers. Many little girls grew up with a natural appreciation of their mothers' skill, and the belief that they too could create works of art.

Many of these samplers featured the alphabet or a pious or sentimental verse, and the name and birthplace of the child who stitched it. Floral patterns were also popular, and many children worked their family genealogies, weaving in human hair as a distinctive personal touch.

Because of a dearth of books in pioneer times, particularly books on sewing, the samplers served as pattern books of mending, darning, buttonholing, cross-stitching, embroidery, and hemming. The carefully worked letters would also help prepare the young girl to later mark her sheets and table linen, as well as to read the alphabet. Often the pioneer child would "recite" her ABCs with her needle. Ambitious little girls added personal flourishes—a picture of a horse or other pet animal or a lovely border of flowers and birds. Working a sampler was an art that took time to learn and even more time to do. It was a child's investment in the future. And even more importantly, it helped the child learn that she had something to give—that what she created had value for others.

Of course, not every little girl was gifted

in needlework. There must have been some active, lively little girls who rebelled against such sedentary and tedious work, who found the hours spent in sewing boring and frustrating. Such children were likely reminded by their mothers of the warning given in Ecclesiastes 10:18, "... through idleness of the hands the house droppeth through," or the folk-saying, "An idle mind is the devil's workshop."

Apart from embroidered alphabets, some of the most interesting features of the samplers were the verses used for motifs. Copied from old hymnbooks or the works of early poets, the verses used often seemed rather stern or morose: "My thoughts on awful subjects ran./Damnation and the dead./What horrors seize the guilty soul/ Upon a dying bed." Other typical verses included:

Give me an hour to call my own
Family and friends to make it a home
Love and kindness that ne'er will depart
Enough to fill a thankful heart.

This is our home
The door opens wide
And welcomes you
To all inside!

They whisper to me thou art false
I would fain believe it not
Although thou mayest be all they say
Thou will never be by me forgot.

Other sentiments included these: "Holiness to the Lord," "Absent but not forgotten," "God bless our Happy Home," "Welcome All," "Rock of Ages, Cleft for Me." (Mary Evans, "Museum Samplers," *Woman's Day,* May 1971, p. 108.)

A pioneer child's recollection of her time spent making samplers is recorded for us: "Aunt Nancy reeled the silk from some of the cocoons and dyed the skeins which we used for our art work. These we put in suitable frames, so for years the Lord's Prayer, the Ten Commandments and 'God Bless Our Home' were ever before us."

The diary relates: "At that time our town was frequently visited by people who solicited for a class in music, elocution, or art work. We hardly had to ask twice for the privilege to join these classes. From these art classes our homes became decorated with ... mottoes, which were worked on perforated cardboard and framed. My sister, Sarah, worked the Ten Commandments. I chose the Lord's Prayer. This art work was done with homemade silk floss which we made in Farmington." (Tanner, *A Mormon Mother,* pp. 45-44.)

HARDANGER

Hardanger work was an important part of the traditional embroidery practiced by the pioneers. This type of embroidery, of Scandinavian origin and named for a village in Norway, was characterized by a geometric design worked over counted threads. It was

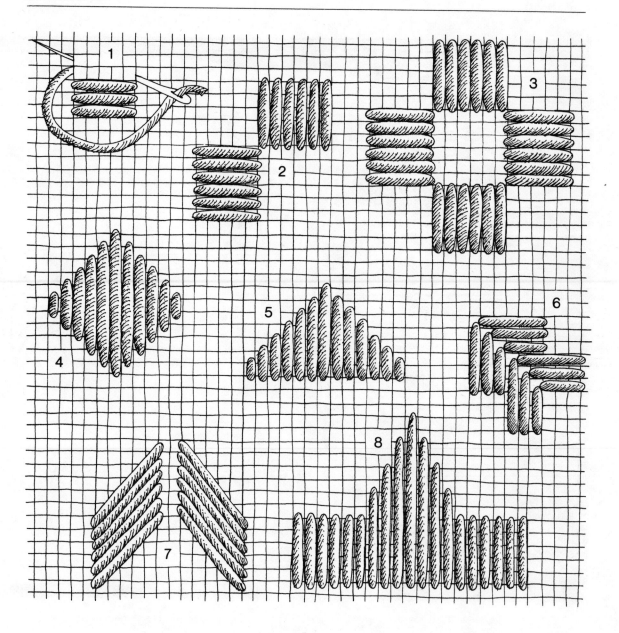

often used in curtain hangings and table coverings.

In hardanger embroidery, the two principal foundation stitches are the satin (kloster) stitch used for the solid parts of the design and the bars worked over the loose threads of the drawn thread spaces. Satin stitches must always be worked before any of the fabric threads are cut or withdrawn. This stitch may be worked from right to left or left to right. The number of threads over which the stitch is worked may vary in depth and length according to the requirements of the design. The stitches are worked between the threads of the fabric. (Fig. 1.)

Horizontal and vertical blocks are used to outline the pattern of the openwork. These blocks consist of seven stitches worked over a square of six fabric threads, with six threads missed between each block except at corners. (Fig. 2.)

Blocks may be worked over more or fewer fabric threads according to the requirements of the design. For example, if 12 threads are to be cut, 13 satin stitches will be worked over 12 threads of fabric. The number of fabric threads missed between the longer blocks may be varied according to the requirements of the design. (Fig. 3.)

Diamonds have varying numbers of stitches, depending on the size required. The diamond shown commences over two threads, increasing two threads with each successive stitch to the center—i.e., 2, 4, 6, 8, 10, and 12 threads—then decreasing two threads each stitch to complete. (Fig. 4.)

The size of pyramids may be varied. The pyramid shown commences over two threads and increases one thread each successive stitch to the center stitch over eight threads, then decreases one thread each stitch to complete. Pyramids may advance two threads with each stitch instead of with one thread. (Fig. 5.)

A mitred shape is produced from satin stitch horizontal and vertical with stitches worked into the same places at the center. (Fig. 6.)

The sloping satin stitch results when the satin stitch is worked obliquely over the fabric threads. (Fig. 7.)

A satin stitch and pyramid is achieved when a regular satin stitch is worked with a pyramid, increasing and decreasing two threads. (Fig. 8.)

Tatting

Tatting was another popular skill of the pioneer women, who spent many quiet hours watching a sleeping baby or sick adult as she worked the shuttle skillfully back and forth and tied the knots that made the exquisite designs. A lace-like knotted threadwork made by hand with a shuttle, tatting was especially beautiful, strong, and durable. Slipping back and forth through the loops, the shuttle tied and secured a lacy pattern of loops, rings, and picots. Tatted articles were useful as doilies, table covers, and scarves, and tatted lace trimmings enriched baby clothes, handkerchiefs, shirts, pillowcases, petticoats, hand towels, and bodices. The tool used, a tatting shuttle, was made of steel, bone, or tortoise shell; special thread was also required.

The art of tatting is still practiced today by careful craftswomen who appreciate the knowledge of their grandparents. Tatting is more intricate and difficult to learn than other kinds of needlework, yet many women today enjoy making the exquisite lace just as their grandmothers and great-grandmothers did. Good instruction books are listed in the bibliography for those interested in learning this skill.

Needlepoint

Needlepoint is another centuries-old form of handwork that was passed down through the generations to the pioneer artists. It was used in pioneer times, as now, to create sturdy fabrics that withstand wear for many years. Needlepoint was especially practical and useful for chair seats, cushion covers, chair-arm covers, footstools, piano stools, book covers, and wall hangings.

In pioneer times needlepoint was done on any available backing, including canvas, duck, and heavy duty muslin. Burlap and other woven fabrics were used when they were available.

Needlepoint is a classical art, exacting and limited in its variations, but pioneer needle workers had an endless variety of patterns from which to choose. It was necessary for them to outline their chosen design on the backing itself before they began their stitching. The yarns used were, of necessity, home-dyed until commerce brought yarns from the East. A tapestry needle, characterized by a large eye and blunt tip, was necessary for efficient needlepoint work. Three varieties of needlepoint were used:

1. Petit point, which is worked in tiny stitches on a tight mesh canvas.

2. Gros point, which is worked on a large mesh canvas using very thick yarn, and which works up rapidly and is quick and easy to do. Petit point and gros point are always worked at an angle or diagonal, always crossing an intersection or a number of intersections.

3. Bargello (Florentine) needlepoint, which is worked vertically in shades of colors as in the popular flame stitch. Bargello has an endless number of variations, and any number of holes may be skipped for a design. Almost any evenly woven fabric can be used for bargello.

Most of the needlepoint stitches are variations of either a slanting or a vertical stitch. The slanting stitch covers one intersection of canvas threads, and the straight stitch is worked up and down over the horizontal threads. The great variety of stitches comes from working these two simple stitches over varying numbers of threads or intersections in different combinations and sequences. The traditional or basic stitches in needlepoint are the basket-weave stitch, continental stitch, and the half-cross stitch. The illustrations show some of the more popular needlepoint stitches used by the pioneer craftsman.

Needlepoint canvas is woven with spaced threads with holes for the needle and yarn to pass through and is available in single mesh and double mesh in a wide variety of widths. The coarseness of the canvas is determined by the threads or mesh to the inch. The range is 3 to 28, with 28 being the finest. Single mesh or mono canvas consists of single threads evenly spaced. Double mesh or penelope canvas is woven with pairs of threads, each pair being counted as one for gros point. For petit point, the threads are separated with the needle and worked singly, doubling the number of stitches to the inch.

Needlepoint canvases are available for today's artisan in a wide variety of custom designs and patterns. Hand-painted canvases are expensive, but it is fairly simple to create original designs. In coloring canvas, be sure to use only permanent markers; otherwise, the colors may run into the yarn during blocking.

Although many types of yarns and canvases are available, 3-ply Persian wool is the best yarn, and a good quality canvas is necessary. Canvas comes in two types, penelope and mono, available in a variety of sizes of mesh. Tapestry needles also come in various sizes to correspond with the size of the mesh to be used.

Crocheting

Crocheting and knitting were other needlecrafts employed by the pioneers in providing

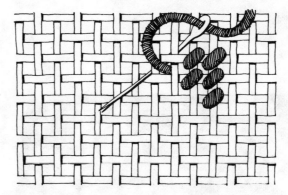

BASKETWEAVE

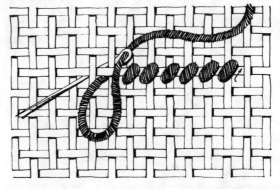

CONTINENTAL

HALF - CROSS

articles of wearing apparel for their families. Baby clothing, outer garments, bed covers, tablecloths, and many other articles were crocheted. Crocheted lace was a favorite trimming and edging for hand-sewn garments. It is faster and less difficult to make than "bobbin" laces, and requires only a crochet hook and thread. Bobbin lace uses a set of bobbins or spools to create the lace pattern and is more intricate, requiring great skill.

All the natural fibers that were available in pioneer times—wool, silk, cotton, and linen—were used in crochet work. Much crocheted lace was elegant and beautiful. It was used for trimming table linens, sheets, pillow cases, children's clothing, and women's petticoats and undergarments.

One of the favorite crocheted articles found in the pioneer home was the afghan or crocheted coverlet done in the easy and popular granny stitch. This colorful pattern is ideal for using up scraps of yarn. Instructions for crocheting a granny square afghan, mittens, scarves, pillow covers, dresses, blouses, and purses can be found in many crocheting instruction books today.

Knitting

Knitting, known since ancient times, is one of the oldest handcrafts. Many pioneer women brought their knitting knowledge and skills with them from Puritan New England or from the German or Scandinavian countries of the

Old World. Yarn ranged from the heavy wool used for making stockings to the fine threads used in lace making. Many little children learned to knit before they learned to read, and in school the clicking of knitting needles was often intermingled with the reading of the ABCs.

Almost all the stockings worn by the pioneers were knit by hand by the women of the family. Fine yarn was doubled and twisted by respinning, and was used to make women's stockings and scarves as well as men's socks. The men's socks were generally made of natural gray and white wool, with the top six inches purled in white yarn. The heels and toes were also white. Later, wools were dyed various colors, and sometimes the colored yarns were twisted together to knit stockings of colorful hues. Hand-knit stockings had good wearing qualities. When a hole appeared it was darned, redarned, and darned again. Later on, cotton became available and replaced much of the wool used for ordinary wear.

Knitting also produced an endless array of caps, gloves, scarves, sweaters, mittens, head covers, shawls, and even petticoats. Every pioneer woman was, of necessity, an experienced and skillful knitter, using needles made by the pioneer craftsmen from the wood available. Later, steel or metal needles were shipped in and supplanted some of the wooden needles. Instructions for knitting mittens, sweaters, scarves, and other articles are available today in many needlework departments.

CHAPTER FIVE

QUILTS

One of the most facinating and necessary pioneer home arts was quilt making. Women worked at home and at quilting bees, combining work and pleasure to produce beautiful quilts, many of which reflected their thoughts, hopes, and ideals.

The first quilts in the West were brought by the pioneers with their scant belongings from the eastern United States or the Old World. As these quilts wore out, others were made. New fabrics, which had to be shipped in or made at home, were too expensive to use for common bedding. One pioneer journal mentions a beautiful quilt in a double-star pattern that cost $1.00 a yard for the bleached material and 60 cents a yard for the green calico. Another quilt was made of calico that cost $1.50 a yard and of quilting thread at $1.00 a spool. (Laura P. Angell King, in *Heart Throbs of the West*, vol. 2, pp. 483-84.)

Since the pioneers' incomes were very limited, quilts were usually made of scraps of fabric left over from used clothing and other household articles. Often some of the materials that went into these early quilts had previously been part of a cloak or shawl, a woolen petticoat or flannel shirt. When the garments could no longer be worn, they were cut apart and the usable pieces sewn together in random designs to make the top of a quilt. The familiar pieced patchwork quilt was thus designed to serve economic needs as well as to satisfy the need for creative and colorful home furnishings.

Quilts were the intensely personal creation of their makers, as their feelings for line,

STAR OF BETHLEHEM

form, and color were expressed in their patchwork. Designs ranged from plain, ordinary coverlets to elegant creations made of beautiful fabrics and stitched with exquisite embroidery. But whatever the mode or the manner, the intrinsic beauty resulted primarily from the skill, craftsmanship, and sensitivity of the quiltmaker.

The simplest and most common quilts were constructed of even, geometric shapes. The easiest were those using the square patch as a base. These and other shapes were cut from a pattern called a template. Exact cutting was necessary.

Simple squares of fabric were joined together in blocks and sections small enough to work on easily. When enough blocks to cover a bed were ready, they were assembled or set into a quilt top. An endless variety was possible with small squares of brightly colored calico in basic combinations of four or nine patches, or blocks of tiny squares joined with larger ones in interesting chain effects.

The triangle, cut from a basic square, formed the pattern for many designs, including Pine Tree, Birds in Flight, Wild Goose Chase, and Bear Claw. The diamond shape, which required much skill in cutting and accuracy in piecing to keep the points fine, became the basis for the many simple or elaborate star patterns, such as the familiar Sunburst, Lemoyne, Lemon Star, and Star of Bethlehem. The most difficult of all shapes to assemble were the curved ones of circles, ovals, or parts of circles.

Pieced quilts were the most popular

kinds among pioneer homemakers, and one of the best-loved pieced quilts was called the friendship quilt, frequently made by a group of friends, with each girl or woman making an individual block. The blocks were usually different in design, fabric, or workmanship, each sample showing the maker's distinctive talent. The blocks were often individual treatments of a specific theme, such as a motto, scriptural quotation, religious subject, or patriotic symbol. Sometimes each friend would sign her name in indelible ink or in outline stitch on the separate blocks. When the blocks were finished, they were assembled and quilted by the group. These quilts were highly prized and often given as wedding presents. They were also called album quilts.

The names the pioneers and their predecessors gave to their multipatterned quilts were quite as colorful and individual as the women who made them. Sometimes the name was descriptive of the design, but often it was reminiscent of people, places, or historical events. Naming the quilt was a part of the quilting culture, and sometimes a certain pattern would have a series of names, depending on the area and background of the particular place where the quilter lived.

For example, the familiar Log Cabin quilt was called in various parts of the country such descriptive names as Courthouse Steps, Straight Furrow, Barn Raising, Lincoln's Platform, and Jacob's Ladder. Another quilt with a series of blocks set at an angle was called Baby Blocks, Tea Boxes, Pandora's

SUNBURST

TREE OF LIFE

CRAZY QUILT

Box, Tumbling Blocks, and Heavenly Steps.

The six-pointed star pattern was adaptable to many variations of composition as well as name. It was known as Blazing Star, Rolling Star, and Chained Star. The eight-pointed star had even more names. It was the Star of LeMoyne, corrupted in New England to Lemon Star, in Texas to the Lone Star of Texas, and in the West, the California Star. Some pioneers called it the Rising Sun, Sunburst, and even Sunflower.

The quilt pattern with the name Delectable Mountain, taken from John Bunyan's *Pilgrim's Progress*, became Kansas Troubles, or Missouri Troubles in the Midwest. The familiar Bear's Paw pattern was also called Duck's Foot in the Mud and the Hand of Friendship.

A variety of names for one popular colonial quilt pattern included Pine Tree, Live Oak, Temperance, Paradise, and Christmas Tree.

Other names show the romance of quilt titles: Basket of Flowers, Grandmother's Farm, Odd Fellow's Patch, Wheel of Fortune, Wedding Ring, Flower Garden, Pennsylvania Hex, Greenfield Village, Triple Irish Chain, Old Maid's Ramble, Storm at Sea, Bear's Tracks, Turkey's Track, Rose of Sharon, Wild Goose Chase, Friendship Medley, Hexagon

KANSAS TROUBLES

LEMON STAR

Beauty, Roman Stripe, and Windmill Blades.

Requiring greater skill than the early pieced quilts were the appliqued or "laid on" patchwork ones, in which shapes were cut from one fabric and then skillfully sewn to a contrasting background. When quilted, the applique was especially beautiful, because the tiny quilting stitches highlighted the applique and made it stand out in bold relief. The skilled quiltmaker usually filled in the empty spaces with intricate designs and motifs to show off her needlework.

Appliqued quilts were usually made from new cloth when fabrics became available in greater quantities. They were more costly to make and therefore generally saved for special occasions, such as visits by important guests, holidays, or family events. They were also treasured wedding gifts.

A familiar, well-loved pioneer quilt that employed applique was the sunbonnet quilt, which took its theme from the sunbonnet worn by pioneer women and children as they crossed the plains and worked or played in the early settlements. The name of the pattern sometimes varied from place to place. It was occasionally called Dutch Children, Sunbonnet Children, or Sunbonnet Sue.

For each sunbonnet quilt, boy and girl patterns were cut out in a variety of colors and

appliqued to solid-colored blocks. The blocks were then sewn together to make the size of quilt desired. The pattern was especially popular for children's and babies' quilts.

Another popular appliqued quilt was called the Crazy Quilt, made from a hodgepodge of sizes and shapes of fabric pieces. Often rich fabrics of silk, satin, velvet, fine wool, or brocade were used. It followed no discernible pattern but was put together at random, letting the shape of the pieces determine the construction. A thin fabric backing was used to hold the scraps or "crazy blocks" in shape. Any size fabric scrap could be used except very large pieces. Unusual shapes added interest to the overall pattern of the quilt. The Crazy Quilt was most attractive if the pieces were chosen within a complementary color range, but this was not always possible in frugal households. The size and shape of the blocks determined the quilt design.

The pieces were pinned to the backing with every visible raw edge turned under except selvage edges. When the backing was covered by the pieces of fabric, each piece was stitched in place with feather stitching for a decorative quilt or with plain stitching for conventional quilting. A crazy quilt top was often combined with a flannel back. These layers and a light batting were either quilted with medium stitches or tied together.

Pioneer women usually had a number of quilt tops on hand and at least one in the making. Taught from childhood to fashion quilt blocks and patchwork tops from the family scrapbag, every young girl had in her dowry several quilt tops for daily use, ready to be made up when she established her own home. After her marriage, she continued to replenish her supply as family needs expanded.

The piecing of the quilt top was usually "pick-up work," done between household chores or in precious leisure moments. But the quilting itself was usually a group effort and was often an excuse for a party or a social gathering. The quilting bee was a time-honored event that combined work and pleasure. In pioneer times, bees were held for any work that required several hands—corn husking, peach cutting, barn raising, harvesting, or apple paring—but the most popular of all was the quilting bee. On winter days when roads were covered with snow and outdoor tasks were at a minimum, bob sleighs would bring groups of friends together. The women would come in their nicest, freshest dresses and happily spend the hours together working, stitching, exchanging news and gossip, recipes and remedies, and enjoying the company of seldom-seen friends. Working diligently, they would frequently complete the quilting of an entire top in a single day.

Before the quilting bee, the quilt owner would draw the pattern on a plain back (tailor's chalk is used today for this process), if the quilting blocks were not to be followed for the pattern. The layers of the quilt—top, batting, and back—were carefully placed on a rectangular wood frame (a standard item in pioneer homes), stretched tightly, and firmly fastened with clamps to the corners of the frame. The frame was usually supported on chair backs or sawhorse legs.

The women would sit at the sides of the frame and work from the outside in, rolling the quilt frames as sections of the outer portion were finished. When the last stitch had been put in, the quilt was removed from the frame and bound by hand, and the quilting bee would end with a happy party. Husbands, sons, and friends would arrive to admire the finished product, eat a hearty supper, and join in the singing, dancing, or other entertainment.

Truly, those cherished quilts of long ago captured in bright patchwork the life and times of pioneer days. A wonderful description of quilting and how it reflected and permeated the lives of pioneer women is expressed in the thoughts of one homemaker and philosopher:

How much piecin' a quilt is like livin' a life! Many times I've set and listened to Parson Page preachin' about free will, and I've said to myself, "If I could jest git up there in the pulpit with one of my quilts, I could make

life a heap plainer than parson's makin' it with his big words."

You see, to make a quilt, you start out with jest so much caliker; you don't go to the store and pick it out and buy it, but the neighbors give you a piece here and there and you'll find you have a piece left over every time you've cut out a dress, and you jest take whatever happens to come.

But when it comes to cuttin' out the quilt, why, you're free to choose your own pattern. You give the same kind of pieces to two persons and one'll make a "Nine-Patch" and the other one'll make a "Wild-Goose-Chase" and so there'll be two quilts made of the same kind of pieces but jest as different as can be. That's the way of livin'. The Lord sends us the pieces; we can cut 'em out and put 'em together pretty much to suit ourselves. There's a heap more in the cuttin' out and the sewin' than there is in the caliker. (Eliza Calvert Obenchain, *Aunt Jane of Kentucky* [Boston: Little, Brown & Co., 1910].)

How to Quilt

To speed work, use a short needle especially made for quilting. Also use quilting thread; it is strong and smooth and less likely to knot. If quilting thread is not available, dual-duty polyester thread may be used. Use a short length of thread when beginning; pull the knot through to the batting so it will not show. Place the forefinger of the left hand over the spot where the needle should come through, and push the needle through with the right hand until it touches the finger. Change hands, and pull the needle through with the right hand. The forefinger should now be underneath. With the right hand, push the needle down through the three layers to touch the forefinger; then pull it through with the right hand. Work alternately in this fashion. Fasten the end of each thread securely by back stitching. Up and down movement through layers is the only correct way to quilt. [See illustrations, right]

Binding a Quilt

Cut enough bias strips of the desired width to go around the entire quilt edge. For a ¼" finished binding cut the strips 1" wide; for a ½" finished binding, cut strips 1½" wide; for a ¾" finished binding, 2" wide. (This allows ¼" seam allowance on each edge of the binding.)

Join all strips together in one continuous strip of material. With right sides together, pin or baste the binding on the edge of the quilt top. Machine stitch in place. Turn under ¼" seam allowance on the other edge of the binding and fold over to the back side of quilt. Blind stitch in place over the machine stitching. If quilt corners are rounded, this bias binding will go around nicely, but if the corners are square, it will be necessary to miter the four corners of the binding.

Sometimes quilts are self-bound by turning in the edges of the top and bottom layers ½" and pinning them together. They are then stitched together with small or blind stitches.

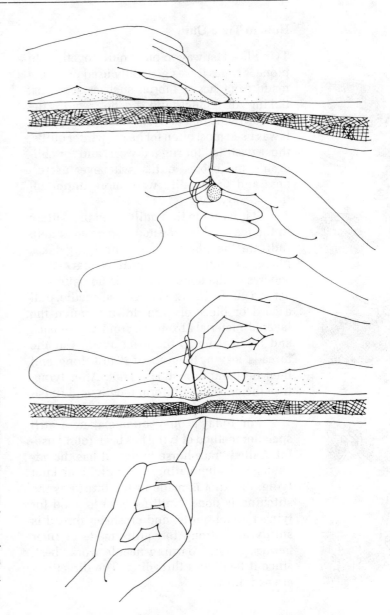

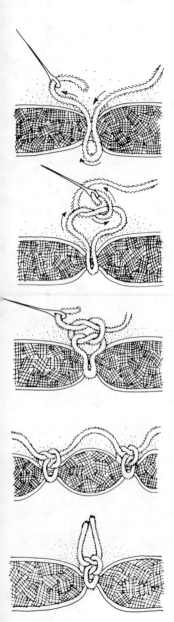

How to Tie a Quilt

Tying is a fast way to put a quilt together. In pioneer times it was generally used on quilts made from heavy fabric, such as woolens, ticking, or flannel, and did not require the tedious hours that conventional quilting did. It was used most often for heavy winter quilts, those destined for rugged wear, and for children's and babies' quilts, whenever usefulness and practicality were more important than beauty.

It is easier to tie a quilt when the pattern in the material is repeated; the designs help indicate the places where the tying takes place. Sometimes the quilt is marked in squares or diamonds if there is no pattern to act as a guide. Using a large-eyed needle, pull a cord or piece of yarn down through the layered materials from the front to the back and bring it up to the front again. Cut the threads, leaving them about 2" to 3" long, and then tie them in a square knot. After tying, trim the ends to a uniform length, and finish the quilt by binding the edges.

For today's busy homemaker, a still speedier method of tying has been found useful. Called "race-horse tying," it has the advantage of eliminating the individual knot tying; the knot is made in the thread as the stitching is done. Knitting yarn is good for tying flannel quilts, and crosheen thread is sturdy and strong for quilts made of finer fabrics. A large darning needle works best, since it facilitates threading. The directions are as follows:

Step 1. At the beginning point, and working through quilt fabric and bat, take a small stitch at a 45° angle.

Step 2. Tie a square knot by looping the left yarn (in needle) above and under the right yarn.

Step 3. Tie a second knot by again bringing the needle yarn from below and up under the right yarn. Pull tight to secure knot.

Step 4. Without cutting the yarn, repeat the stitch at the next point for the knot.

Step 5. When the row is finished, cut the yarn to the desired length between knots. Rows may be worked straight across the quilt or diagonally between rows.

The illustrations show each of these steps.

Trapunto Quilting

Another kind of quilting was trapunto, used for coverlets, furniture covers, and handsome skirts and dresses. It was done with only two layers of cloth and no general padding between layers except in the raised pattern between stitching. Designs of flowers and leaves were drawn on linen and sewn to coarsely woven fabric with outline stitches. Then the work was turned over, and from the back small bits of cotton or wool were pushed through the lining to pad each tiny leaf. With a bodkin, cord was drawn into the lining along each stem. The result was a beautiful raised design that caught light and shadow, highlighting the handwork of the artist.

CHAPTER SIX

PATCHWORK

The frugal habit of salvaging every scrap of precious fabric plus the ingenious ability to "make do" brought patchwork sewing into the forefront of homemaking skills for the pioneer woman. The result of this patching together small pieces to make a whole was often the most colorful article to be found in the log cabin or adobe farm house.

Patchwork aprons, pillows, quilts (either to cover a bed or to hang over a door or window to keep out the cold), chair covers, sewing bags, skirts, table covers, and rugs were common in the pioneer home and provided a dual outlet for the homemaker. The free-form patterns allowed her to exercise her artistic imagination and also afforded some practical uses for the inevitable collection of scraps.

Brigham Young, prophet-president of the Mormon Church in pioneer times, said, "Sisters, gather up the rags—those little fine pieces that you have been throwing about and sew them together, and make nice petticoats and aprons for little girls, coverlets, etc. and then teach them to do it themselves, that they may here-after make good wives."

That the pioneers heeded this advice is evident from the many household articles that appeared in pioneer homes as a result of "piecing." As Brigham Young knew, cloth was too scarce and expensive to waste, so every odd-shaped snippet of calico or chintz was saved to be stitched together to make a larger piece of material in a Crazy Patch.

It was not long before women, craving beauty and order, began to plan their piecework. The haphazard Crazy Patch was succeeded by a number of carefully planned arrangements of design in which each piece was trimmed to the same size and shape and then put together in some deliberate order. One of these was called Roman Stripe, so called because of the alternating dark and light colors used. From their first attempts at planned patchwork, these ingenious women went on to more creative and elaborate designs: stars, sunbursts, trees, flowers of all kinds, wreaths, sea scallops, and many other well-known shapes. The geometric arrangements were unlimited. Using squares, triangles, circles, rectangles, diamond shapes, and other forms, pioneer women created unlimited variations on a familiar theme.

It was a matter of pride with many of them to never copy the exact pattern of another friend or neighbor. Rather, the seamstress would adapt a basic pattern to her own artistic nature and come up with a new design. Thus, there came from each basic motif countless variations.

The pioneer women were not merely frugal and obedient; they were also daring, imaginative, and highly individualistic. Their patchwork heritage is a testimony to the spirit that conquered the western wilderness and that created out of it homes of beauty and strength. There was time enough to work out intricate designs, for piecing was a lonely as well as exacting pastime. Looking at the variety of patterns they produced inspires curiosity about those women who sat through the isolated hours snipping and stitching, taking pride in their meticulous work, finishing one piece and then another, dreaming perhaps of the completed article that would bring joy to their daughters, themselves, and their household.

Patchwork was a versatile craft, and the variety of objects produced testifies to its popularity. One of the favorite uses was the patchwork or appliqued wall hanging. Farm houses, rolling hills, groves of trees, flower gardens, and animals were popular subjects. Tiny scraps were cut out to fit the design and then mounted or appliqued with great skill to the chosen background material, usually a gingham or calico print. Often embroidered details were added for a more artistic effect. These lovely old landscapes and garden-scapes or portraits are highly treasured in homes where they have been preserved and handed down from generation to generation. A few rare ones have found their way into museums, where they give incentive to the modern needleworker looking for bygone skills to emulate.

Though the story of patchwork is very old, the craft itself is remarkably relevant to today's world. The patterns are bold, the colors vibrant in their contrasts, and the geometric designs most modern. Patchwork's gaiety fits in naturally with the informal and rather casual life-style of today's modern homemaker. So, although patchwork was introduced by our great-grandmothers, it has become a bridge across the generation gap for many modern homemakers, who now find the same fascinating pleasure in adapting the old patterns to their individual tastes and surroundings as their ancestors did.

Today's seamstresses and craftswomen are piecing together attractive and colorful articles of clothing, many of which are seen in the most expensive couturier shops and boutiques. The fashion-minded woman of today can apply the same skills as her grandmother did and create her own beautiful pieced skirts, hostess aprons, tote bags, decorative art-nouveau pillows, wall hangings, children's clothing, toys, tablecloths, place mats, and decorative accessories. All she needs to do is look in her scrap bag and begin to snip and stitch, piece and patch, to put together an original creative item.

Instructions for making a patchwork apron or skirt are simple. Simply cut squares of the desired size and sew them together to form strips of the desired length. Then sew the strips together to form a large piece of material. For a skirt, stitch the seams, gather the material at the waist, and add a waistband. Then insert a zipper at the back or left side seam and hem at the correct length.

For an apron, gather the patchwork, add a waistband with extended ties at the top, and hem the edges and bottom.

Decorator pillows can be made in a bright array of colors, patterns, and fabrics. Elegance is achieved by using velvets, corduroys, satins, or silks. Patchwork pillows made with ribbons stitched or appliqued to velvet fabric are very popular. It is usually best if the material is all the same type—don't mix cottons with wool or polyester, or silk and velvet with gingham or homespun. Pillows may be made by using a large pieced quilt block for the front and adding a complementary back. They are most practical if the outside is removable and finished with a zipper opening. The pillow itself can be made of muslin or inexpensive fabric and stuffed with foam rubber, dacron batting, or any of the commercial stuffings on the market. Goose down and feathers such as our grandmothers used are no longer available, but the products on the market are washable and lightweight and make good substitutes.

Patchwork tablecloths, place mats, runners, and table skirts are made by the same piecing and patching method. Be sure the fabrics and colors are suitable, complementary, and attractive. Table coverings can be made from elegant tapestry and brocade scraps and trimmed with expensive braids, or they can be made from the least expensive cottons and ginghams in gay cottage prints and colors. The variety is endless and is limited only by what the scrap bag can produce and the creator can design.

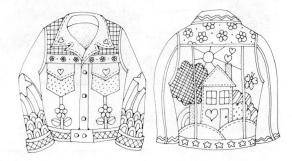

CHAPTER SEVEN

DYEING

Most pioneer women were hundreds of miles from any source of fabric dye. When dyes were available, they were usually priced prohibitively high, so much of the material for clothing and household articles was not dyed.

However, the pioneer women longed for colors. Friendly Indians told them about shrubs and plants they used for dyeing and the sand they used as a coloring agent in their paints. But in most cases the inventive and curious homemakers discovered their own dyes. Rabbit brush, sagebrush, the creosote plant, and chaparral all contributed colors.

Discovering plants for dyeing was an adventure in itself, and many pioneer craftswomen found the same delight in discovering something new as did the Indian basketmaker who found in the purple iris a dye almost as deep in color as the iris blossoms.

The pioneers found that the best time to gather vegetable materials for dye making was in the fall or late autumn when the seeds were fully ripened. Knowing just how much bark or other material to use to dye properly came only by experiment and practice. One pioneer authority wrote: "Butternut bark, walnut shucks, sumac, pokeberries, onion skins and so on—all that can be held in both hands, a little more will do no harm." (Mary Atwater, *Shuttlecraft Book of American Hand Weaving* [New York: Macmillan Co., 1951], p. 76.)

After settlements were established, a great deal of time and expense went into producing natural dyes. Brigham Young encouraged the raising of madder and indigo, which were expensive to import.

Occasionally some of the ingredients used in dyeing were poisonous and needed to be handled with great care. Others had unpleasant effects on the skin, so it was always safer and more expedient to handle dyestuffs with a wooden paddle or a pair of forked sticks.

Some of the most revealing and informative stories about pioneer coloring can be found in old journals and newspaper articles. Consider the account given by John R. Banes:

"In a covered barrel that we kept outside on purpose we would accumulate all the wine we could save until it was half full and [add to] it a woolen bag filled with indigo. We sould stir it with a long stick. Then we would put our wool into the barrel and every morning hold it up with a stick to let it get fresh air. When [the wool] was dark, we would put it into tubs of fresh water until it was clean, and finally we would wash it with soap and water. It was true blue and never faded." (Helen Lamprecht, "Textile Arts of the Mormon Pioneers," master's thesis, Oregon State University, 1965, p. 33.)

Many fabrics and fibers took to dyeing with great ease. Others were less responsive. Linen was a fiber that was extremely resistant to dyes, and to get the strong, darker colors on linen, it was sometimes necessary to use equal weights of yarn and dye. Since this was expensive and time-consuming, and since the natural color of linen is so beautiful in

itself, it was easier to use the material in its natural state or to bleach it white and leave color to cottons, wool, and other materials.

Before the actual dyeing process began, a mordant was used to set the dye. The cloth to be dyed was soaked in the mordant, which later combined with the dye to create a lasting color. Wood ash alkali was the most common mordant, but alum, cream of tartar, sal ammonia, verdigris, and copperas were also used. Alum was practical because it was so easily obtained. Different recipes were used for mixing the mordant; one of the best called for three ounces of alum dissolved in one quart of water. After the mordant was used, the material was soaked in water and wrung out, then placed in the dye bath.

It took about half an hour of good boiling for most dyes to give their color, though some dyes, such as cochineal, took two full hours to produce the best results. The dye was steamed in a huge brass or copper kettle over an open fire. The dye solution covered the material completely, although part of the goods could be wrapped in cornhusks to vary color intensity.

The dye was kept boiling and the material was stirred frequently to prevent streaking. When the desired color was reached, the material was removed from the kettle, rinsed in cold water until no more color came off, then hung on outdoor lines or bushes, where it flapped in the wind until dry.

RECIPES FOR DYEING

A number of pioneer recipes for dyeing follow. These were written down in old notebooks and household records. The directions given will act as suggestions for the modern craftswoman. Some of them use dyes and chemicals that were purchased commercially rather than produced at home.

BLUE Powdered indigo was an important item in pioneer times. It had to be imported and was fairly expensive, but no substitute was found to replace it, for the shade it produced was both beautiful and permanent.

Mix 1 pound powdered indigo with water until it is of the consistency of paste, for easier handling. Then dilute it with about 2 quarts water and pour it into a vat outdoors.

Dissolve 2½ pounds copperas in boiling water, and add enough water to cool the liquid. Pour it into the vat with the indigo, stirring thoroughly. Mix 3 pounds slaked lime with ten quarts of water, and pour into the vat, using a wooden rake for stirring. Then add 24 quarts water to the vat, stirring vigorously. Let mixture stand for 48 hours in a moderately warm place. Occasionally stir it vigorously. If the dye turns out well, the liquid will be dark amber in color and will produce a dark blue scum when stirred with the rake. If the liquid is greenish, there is unreduced indigo present, and more copperas is needed. If it is brownish, more lime is required. Therefore, the dye must always be tested for color.

To dye the material, immerse it in the liquid by means of two wooden sticks. Drain. Repeat the process three times. If the color is not deep enough, repeat until the desired shade appears. Rinse thoroughly and dry out of doors.

The *Deseret News* of August 4, 1858, offered the following recipe to dye blue cotton:

"For 5 pounds of clothe take 2 ounces of copperas, put it in water sufficient to cover the clothe; keep it scalding hot for 2 hours, take out the clothe, turn out the copperas water, rinse the kettle, put 1 ounce prussiate of potash in soft water; when dissolved put in the cloth and add 1 spoonful of oil of vitriol, stir it well; then again put in the clothe; let it lie a few minutes, take it out, rinse thoroughly in cold water."

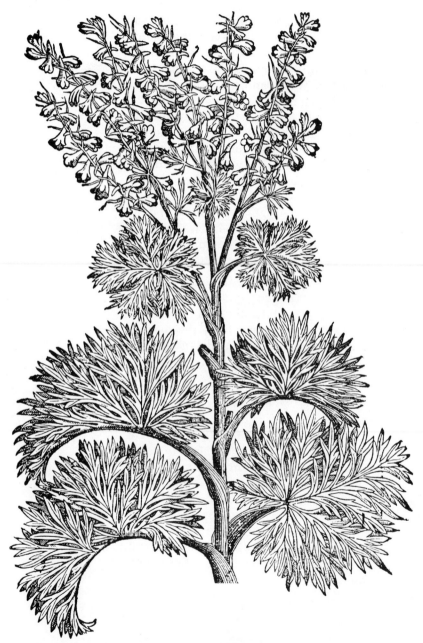

BLUE (Quick Process) Cover two pounds of goods in water in which 5 ounces alum and 3 ounces cream of tartar have been dissolved. Boil for 1 hour. Then put goods in warm water in which a sufficient amount of extract of indigo has been dissolved to make the desired shade. Boil for 30 minutes.

SKY BLUE Dissolve 2 ounces blue vitriol in 1 gallon water. Dip goods for 15 minutes. Rinse in lime water.

LIGHT BLUE Combine the following ingredients: 1 gallon water, 1 glassful sulphuric acid; 2 tablespoons glauber salts in crystals; and 1 teaspoon liquid extract of indigo. Boil the goods about 15 minutes. Rinse in cold water. In pioneer times, spiderwort, wax myrtle, garden purslane, and larkspur also furnished blue dye for yarn or materials.

GREEN 1. Use barley tobacco with blue vitriol, sage, chaparral, creosote bush, black oak bark, or gold seal, combined with indigo.

2. Dye goods with indigo first, then overlay with quercitron yellow.

3. Make a dye bath of 1 pound fustic and 3½ ounces alum, with water to cover 1 pound of goods. Steep until a good yellow is obtained. Remove the chips and add extract of indigo, 1 tablespoonful at a time, until the desired color is obtained.

BLUE-GREEN Use sunflower seeds with blue vitriol.

WINE COLOR For 5 pounds of goods, use 2 pounds camwood in sufficient water to cover goods. Boil water and camwood 30 minutes; add goods, and boil another 30 minutes. Darken with 1½ ounces blue vitriol. If not dark enough, add ½ ounce copperas.

PURPLE For each pound of goods to be dyed, use 2 ounces cudbear. Wet the goods well in soapsuds. Then dissolve the cudbear in hot suds, not quite boiling, and soak the goods until the desired color is reached. The color is brightened by rinsing in alum water.

YELLOW Juniper clippings, goldenrod blossoms, onion skins, Saint-John's-wort, walnut, hickory, yellow oak, Lombardy poplar bark, turmeric, peach leaves, smartweed leaves, sumac stalks, rabbit bush, clematis, alder, and birch bark were all used to obtain a yellow shade.

    1. Recipe using onion skins: Mordant the wool with alum and a little cayenne pepper. Let it boil lightly and keep it warm for about 6 days. Dry the wool. Boil a quantity of onion skins and cool. Put the wool in the kettle, cover with the dye bath, and boil lightly for 30-60 minutes; then keep warm for 1 hour. Wring out and wash.

    2. Quercitron comes in the form of a paste. Place 2 ounces of it in a cotton bag and soak overnight in water. Dissolve ¼ pound washing soda in 1 gallon water. Immerse the goods to be dyed in the water and let stand overnight. In the morning, fill the dye kettle with 4 gallons water and bring to a boil. Pour in the quercitron juice. Place the soaked goods in the kettle and boil for 30 minutes.

RICH YELLOW Stir 5 pounds of goods in a boiling dye bath with 3 ounces bichromate of potash and 2 ounces alum, for ½ hour. Remove the goods, drain, and cool. Make another bath by dissolving 5 pounds fustic in water enough to cover the goods. Boil the cloth in the fustic compound 30 minutes. Wash out and dry.

YELLOW-ORANGE Dragon's blood may be purchased from the druggist in either stick or powdered form. Since alcohol must be used to dissolve the stick, it is best to buy the powder. Tie 2 ounces of the powder in a cheesecloth bag and soak overnight in a quart of cold water. In the morning add 1 gallon warm water. Let the dye bath come to a boil. The material to be dyed must meanwhile have been mordanted.* Put it in the dye bath and boil hard for 30 minutes.

ORANGE For bright orange, use madder with alum. For orange-brown, use dragon's blood. For 5 pounds of goods, combine 6 tablespoons muriate of tin and 4 ounces argol with water to cover goods. Boil 1 hour. Add 1 cup madder liquid. Boil another 30 minutes.

SALMON Combine ¼ pound annatto, ¼ pound scraped soap, and 1 gallon water. Rinse the goods well in warm water, immerse in dye bath, and boil hard for 30 minutes. This will dye 1 pound of goods.

---

*Use this method, which will be referred to as Standard Method: Dissolve 4 ounces powdered alum in 2 gallons water, and soak the material in this mordant for 2 hours.

RED Madder, various berries, cochineal (from Mexico), red arsenic, and Eurasian herbs were used to make red dye. Cranberries and beets give a dull red, while cochineal combined with cream of tartar results in a bright red.

TURKEY RED (From the Journal of Priddy Meeks) Combine 2 ounces cochineal, 1 pound madder, 1 pound red sawdust, 2 ounces alum, 1 ounce red arsenic. Boil 3 hours. Leave 5 gallons of dye in the kettle. Put cloth in the dye 1 hour. Keep the dye warm. This quantity is for 5 pounds of deep turkey red cotton and 4 pounds scarlet wool. (Lamprecht, "Textile Arts of the Mormon Pioneers," p. 22.)

BRIGHT RED This recipe will dye 6 or 7 pounds of rags. Soak 2½ pounds redwood chips overnight in a brass kettle. The next morning add ½ pound powdered alum, and boil to obtain the strength of the chips. Strain the liquid. Add the material to be dyed, and simmer until of the desired shade.

MADDER RED Mordant the goods to be dyed by dissolving 5 ounces alum and 3 ounces cream of tartar in enough water to cover all the material thoroughly. Bring the contents of the dye kettle to a boil, and boil for 30 minutes. Then air the material. Return to the kettle and boil 30 minutes longer. Empty the kettle and fill with clean water. Put in 1 peck bran. Heat and let the liquid stand until the bran rises. Skim off the bran and add ½ pound powdered madder. Heat slowly; strain, and return liquid to dye pot. Put in the material

and boil for 45 minutes. Wash the material in strong suds, rinse thoroughly, and dry.

CLARET Combine 3 gallons water, 12 ounces cudbear, 4 ounces logwood, 4 ounces old fustic, and ½ ounce alum. Boil the goods in the mixture for 1 hour. Wash and rinse the cloth. This will dye 1 to 2 pounds of material.

CRIMSON These ingredients will dye one pound of goods: Mordant goods for 10 minutes in mixture of 4 ounces of powdered alum dissolved in 2 gallons water, 3 ounces paste cochineal, 2 ounces bruised nutgalls, and ¼ ounce cream of tartar. Strain. Return liquid to dye pot, add mordanted goods, and boil for 1 hour. Wash, rinse, and dry material.

BEET RED Use 5 or 6 large beets to a gallon of water. Thoroughly wash the beets and cook them in water until they lose their color. Strain the liquid through cheesecloth. Dissolve 4 ounces of powdered alum in 2 gallons water; then soak the material in this mordant for 2 hours. Heat the beet juice in a kettle until it boils. Immerse the material and boil for 30 minutes, turning the material over and over during the process.

CRANBERRY RED Boil 1 pound cranberries in 1 gallon water until they lose color. Continue as with Beet Red.

COCHINEAL SCARLET Make a bag of cotton cloth and place in it 2 ounces cochineal (grain). Tie a string about the mouth of the bag. Place in a stone crock and cover with cold water. After the coloring matter is drawn

out, fill a dye pot half full of cold water and add to the cochineal 4 ounces oxalic acid, 4 ounces single muriate of tin, and 1 ounce cream of tartar. Boil these ingredients for 10 minutes. Fill the kettle with cold water. Thoroughly wet the goods to be dyed, and place in the kettle. (This rule differs from others in that the dye bath is *not* boiling when the material is first immersed.) Bring the contents of the kettle slowly to a boil. Boil hard for 1 hour, stirring frequently. Take out the goods and rinse in cold water.

BROWNISH RED Squawberry bush is the dye ingredient.

BROWN Burdock, walnuts, barks of butternut tree, hemlock, and maple.

BROWN (made from scaly moss) Here is one old recipe: "The scaly moss from rocks and ledges is a good material for coloring brown. Gather the moss and place it in a brass kettle, upon which pour cold water; then let it boil on the stove for three or four hours. Skim out the moss, put in the goods, and boil until you have the desired color. It will never fade." (Ella S. Bowles, *Handmade Rugs* [Boston: Little, Brown & Co., 1927], p. 59.)

MANGANESE BROWN Dissolve 2 ounces permanganate of potash in 2 gallons warm water. The resulting liquid will be crimson instead of brown in color. With wooden sticks place the damp goods in the liquid, taking care that all parts are covered. Remove material from the dye bath. Hang on a line outdoors until the material turns brown. The re-

quired shade is obtained by redipping, partly drying, and then redipping. Dry carefully, wash with soap and hot water, and dry again.

SNUFF BROWN For 5 pounds of cloth, use 1 pound camwood in water sufficient to cover goods. Boil camwood and water 15 minutes, then dip the goods for 45 minutes. Remove the goods. Add to the dye bath 2½ pounds fustic. Boil 10 minutes, and dip the goods for 45 minutes. Add 1 ounce blue vitriol and 4 ounces copperas. Dip again for 30 minutes. If not dark enough, add more copperas.

LONDON BROWN This recipe is for 3 pounds of goods. Boil together for 45 minutes ¾ pound camwood, ½ pound logwood, and 1 ounce quercitron bark. Add 2 ounces copperas, and boil the goods for 30 minutes. Rinse thoroughly and dry.

BUTTERNUT BROWN Do not boil, but steep hot for 30 minutes ½ bushel butternut bark. Add goods and steep for 1 hour; then air them out. Add 1 ounce copperas to the liquid and bring it to a boil. Immerse the goods and boil for 30 minutes. If not dark enough, use more copperas. One part butternut bark and one part black walnut bark make a pleasing color. Experiment in the same way with hemlock bark.

CATECHU BROWN Catechu, which is the dried sap of certain East Indian trees, comes in the form of dried paste. Soak 2 ounces catechu overnight in a stone crock. In the morning put the liquid into the dye kettle with 4 gallons boiling water and 1 ounce copperas. Immerse the material to be dyed, and boil for 90 minutes. Make a solution of 1 ounce bichromate of potash to 1 gallon water. Place the goods in this, and allow them to remain for about 5 minutes. Do not wring the material when you remove it from the solution, but allow it to drip until it dries. Wash and dry again.

LIGHT TAN Soak 2 quarts sumac leaves and 1 quart sumac stems overnight in 1 gallon water. In the morning boil for 30 minutes. Mordant material using Standard Method (see footnote, p. 00). Boil for 45 minutes. Wash the goods and dry.

NANKEEN This is a very old recipe: "Fill a five-pail brass kettle with small pieces of white birch bark and water. Let it steep (but do not boil) for 24 hours. Then skim out the bark. Wet the cloth in soapsuds; then put it in the dye, stir well, and air often. When dark enough, dry. Then wash in suds. It will never fade." (Journal of Priddy Meeks, quoted in Lamprecht, "Textile Arts of the Mormon Pioneers," p. 75.)

STRAW COLOR Peach leaves for dyeing may be gathered at any time of year, but they give a better color in the fall. The dye is made by soaking 2 quarts peach leaves in 1 gallon water overnight. In the morning, let the dye-stuff come quickly to a boil, since overboiling gives a brown instead of the desired yellow shade. Place the mordanted material (see Standard Method, p. 00) in the dye bath, and boil for about 30 minutes.

IRON BUFF Thoroughly dissolve ½ pound copperas in 2 gallons warm water. Also dissolve 1 pound soap powder in 2 gallons water. Place the crocks containing these two liquids side by side. Then, using two wooden sticks, place strips of material to be dyed in the copperas solution, taking care that every part of the goods is covered. Remove from the copperas bath and drain. Using the wooden sticks, place the material in the soap-powder solution. Remove and drain. Repeat this process three times. At first a dull greenish yellow will appear, but after the goods are hung to dry outdoors, the color will turn from a greenish to a reddish yellow.

BLACK Use toadstools, squawbush, logwood roots, or bugle weed to make black. Dissolve ¾ ounce bichromate of potash in 3 gallons water. Boil the goods in this for 40 minutes; then wash in cold water. Add 9 ounces logwood extract, 3 ounces fustic, and 1 or 2 drops double oil of vitriol for each 3 gallons of water. Boil for 40 minutes. Rinse in cold water. Dry fabric. This will color from one to two pounds of material.

Today, analine dyes have replaced most of the vegetable dyes used by our ancestors. But with the resurgence of interest in crafts, many women are going back to the independent ways of their grandmothers and experimenting with making their own dyes. The directions above have proven successful and may be used by weavers and dyers of modern times.

CHAPTER EIGHT

PRODUCING CLOTH AND CLOTHING

Heber C. Kimball, a member of the First Presidency of The Church of Jesus Christ of Latter-day Saints in pioneer times, declared, in a gathering of women, "Ladies, we do not want you to tease your husbands for silks, satins, and fine bonnets, but go to work and manufacture your own clothing, and if you will do that, you will do the best thing that you ever did in your lives."

Pioneer women really had no alternative. It was imperative that they provide their own wearing apparel, not only by sewing the clothing, but also producing the material from which the garments were cut. History shows that they did not tease their husbands for silks and satins, but they did something better. They engaged in sericulture—the raising of silkworms—and produced their own silk material, as well as cotton, linen, and wool fabrics.

Silk Production

Silkworm eggs were imported from France and Italy, as were mulberry tree seeds. Almost every woman was encouraged to plant mulberry trees in abundance to provide the leaves necessary to feed the silkworms. For a number of years the raising of silkworms occupied a great deal of time for those who participated in this unusual adventure. The process was tedious and risky and required almost constant attention.

The silkworm eggs were kept at a cool temperature (below 50° F.) in shipping until they reached their destination. Then they

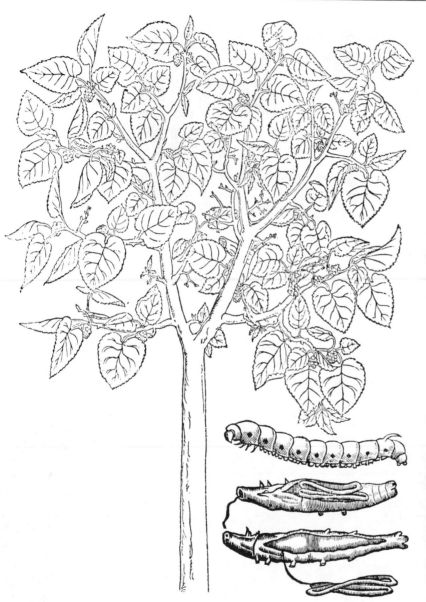

were gradually warmed to a temperature sufficient to hatch the eggs. The eggs were spread on big wooden trays, and the trays were stacked six feet high on hurdles or shelves in a room free of all dust, odors, and disturbing noises. Tobacco was a deadly enemy of the worms, since the fumes would kill them almost immediately. Loud noises, such as the thunder of an electrical storm, could also cause the worms to die.

Since the lifespan of the silkworm was only forty days, with four moulting periods, their growth was rapid. They had voracious appetites for fresh mulberry leaves, which were fed to them three or four times a day. The leaves had to be kept free of any dampness, so in wet weather the leaves were gathered and spread out to dry before being fed to the silkworms.

Perfect cleanliness of the trays was another prerequisite for raising silkworms. At the end of the ten-day moulting period, all the old beds were discarded and clean new trays were provided, with a smaller number of worms than before placed in them to allow sufficient space as they grew larger. Each moulting and cleaning period meant a lot of work for the entire family.

Regular feeding and attentive care resulted in large, even cocoons with a strong thread that was reeled off six days after the process of encasing took place. At the end of the forty-day lifespan of the silkworm, the trays were covered with small branches of scrub oak or rabbit bush, to which the transparent worms attached themselves, and they

were soon encased in their own cocoons. After this process was complete, the cocoons of the largest, most uniform, and earliest maturing were saved to mate and lay eggs for the next year's supply. The rest of the cocoons were heated to a temperature high enough to kill the chrysalides so they would not eat their way out of the cocoons and destroy the continuity of the silk thread.

The cocoons were about the size and shape of a peanut, varying in color from light creamy white to deep yellow. From 500 to 1500 yards of silk could be reeled from a good cocoon. The process of reeling was simple, but it required skill and experience that came only from the earnest application to the work.

Reeled silk was produced by softening the cocoon in hot water, soaking it for a short period, and then brushing it with a stiff brush to remove all broken ends and find the one continuous thread. The strength of the silk fiber was determined by the number of threads combined into one on the bobbin of the reeling machine; the most skillful task of an efficient reeler was to keep the same number of threads continuously on the bobbin. The silk was then removed from the bobbin to a skeiner, which measured the thread. It was then ready for weaving.

Although some cocooneries were started on a commercial basis, the woman working in her home provided most of her own silk thread by painstakingly nursing the silkworms. Hundreds of instances have been cited where women raised from 75 to 100 pounds of cocoons and manufactured the silk

into rich materials for their homes and wearing apparel.

An interesting autobiography tells of the work involved in home sericulture during pioneer times.

I don't know how mother ever spared us to go off and pick the mulberry leaves for the silk worms. I suppose it was because President Young was promoting the silk culture in Utah. Aunt Nancy secured some sheets of paper on which were silk worm eggs, and emptied her rooms to make a place for shelves and scaffolds on which the leaves were spread over the hungry worms. There were some large mulberry trees in Bountiful. A hayrack load of young folks would accompany Aunt Nancy there, where we filled dozens of sacks with the leaves. We took our lunch and for a time we thought it quite a pleasure trip. However, it was hard work to climb those big trees and reach around for the leaves. We were permitted to have some of the branches sawed off. How we scrambled for the easy job to pick from fallen branches! There was a loom in Farmington which made yards of cloth. Sarah and I expected some silk dresses for that hard summer's work, but were disappointed.

Aunt Nancy reeled the silk from some of the cocoons and dyed the skeins which we used for our art work. These we put in suitable frames, so for years the Lord's Prayer, the Ten Commandments and "God Bless Our Home" were ever before us. (Tanner, Autobiography of a Mormon Mother, p. 44.)

Linen

Linen was another natural fiber that the pioneers tried to produce. Early in the history of the westward migration, emigrants from the Scandinavian countries brought many seeds with them. The first flax seeds were brought from Denmark as a medicine, but soon the pioneers who brought the flax seed decided to experiment with growing it in the West, using the same methods they had used in Europe. They constructed toothed wooden brakes to separate the flax fibers from the woody part of the stems. After the flax was prepared, they spun it into thread or twine or wove it into cloth. Linsey woolsey, woven from linen threads lengthwise and from wool crosswise, was a sturdy and popular fabric. In a short time, practically all the tablecloths, sheets, and towels and much of the clothing used by the pioneers were made from flax they had grown.

Linen threads proved resistant to dyeing and also presented some problems in weaving. The linen had to be kept thoroughly damp during the weaving process; it had a great affinity for water, but when it was completely dry it became brittle and lost its elasticity.

Cotton

Cotton growing was another pioneer attempt to augment clothing materials. It was begun in the warm, sunny areas of the Southwest, where the growing season was long. Since

cotton was used as a warp in much of the weaving, it had to be processed. To prepare the raw cotton for spinning, it was carded much like wool, though cotton cards had longer and finer teeth than wool cards. The cotton was then spun on a small wheel. (See the section on wool, page 76, for a more detailed description of carding and spinning.)

Cotton was a profitable commodity for many years, but as commerce improved, the competition of better-grade cotton from more suitable growing areas gradually made it necessary for the pioneers to discontinue the cotton industry in the West. Like silk and

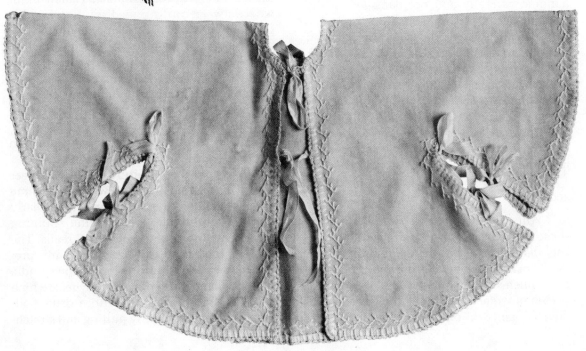

linen production, cotton growing had been discontinued by the turn of the century. Only the production of wool was maintained, and this industry has continued to be one of the major ones in the West, a pioneer heritage that remains today.

Wool

The process of making woolen material began with the raising of sheep, which every pioneer home did for this purpose. The sheep were shared by hand, with much of the shearing being done by the women and teenage girls. Handshearing allowed the fleece to be handled carefully and not damaged in the cutting.

After shearing, the wool was cleaned and prepared, a painstaking process that took much longer than spinning. Sometimes the sheep were taken to the creek and washed before they were sheared, but more often the fleece was scoured and cleaned of all grease after shearing. It was washed and dried with care to preserve and protect the natural softness and elasticity.

A pioneer journal records the following account:

After the wool was sheared from the sheep the women put it in large willow baskets made by men of the community. With these baskets suspended from straps or ropes the women stood on foot bridges over a clear stream of water and dipped the baskets and their contents up and down, up and down until the loose sand and dirt were entirely rinsed from the wool. At this stage they were unable to wash the wool with soap and water as the soap had a tendency to knot it thus preventing it from spinning.

After the rinsing process the wool was spread to dry, usually on the soft green grass. After it was spun into skeins of yarn it was washed in soap and the softest water obtainable, rain water or ordinary water softened with a plant called "oose." This process was called scouring. (Heart Throbs of the West, vol. 2, p. 479.)

After the wool was clean and dry, it was carded. This was done by placing small bits of wool between carding needles—two wooden paddles with rows of fine steel needles on one face of each. The wool was brushed and rolled between the needles until every knot was removed. This was a time-consuming and tedious process, and many a young girl rebelled against the discipline of working the carding needles when she would prefer playing.

After carding, the wool was spun into thread or yarn. The spinning wheel was an important piece of furniture in every pioneer home, and most pioneer women became adept at using it. Each spinner learned early how to control the speed of the spinning wheel and how taut to hold the threads. The spinner took the carded wool (or any prepared fiber) and, spinning it onto the spindle with one hand, turned the large wheel (which kept the spindle turning with a drive belt) with the other, gradually pulling and stretching out the roll while the spindle twisted it into the thread. After she did a few rolls this way, she would turn the wheel and wind the finished thread back on another spindle. Improved spinning wheels were treadle powered, so both hands could feed the wool onto the spindle and more easily control the tension of the thread.

The thread could be spun fine for single use or made into heavier yarn by doubling and respinning it. If the wheel was turned in the opposite direction, the yarn could be twisted to make it stronger. It took a day's time and considerable effort and skill to spin a pound of wool into yarn. In the same amount of time, five or six yards of cloth could be woven.

When the yarn was taken off the spindle of the spinning wheel, it was wound into skeins on a reel, which was somewhat like a tilt-top table topped by a rack, made by crossing two pieces of wood so the four ends were an equal distance from the center. A peg of wood was fastened at the end of each cross bar to hold the yarn in place. As the reel turned, the yarn was measured. It took forty winds of the reel to make one knot of yarn, and ten knots to make one skein. A piece of yarn or twine was tied around each forty winds to keep them separate; in this way, the spinner knew exactly how much yarn had been spun. The yarn was then ready to be dyed, if desired, and used for knitting stockings, mittens, gloves, shawls, and scarves. At this stage it was called finished yarn, or what we today would call as two-ply (two fine threads

doubled and twisted together). Wool that was single spun was called thread and was used to weave cloth. Wool that was to be used for the warp was spun harder and twisted harder than that which was used for weft or woof. Not everyone could make a good warp, so the woman who excelled in this skill was much in demand.

Weaving

For the pioneers, as for their ancestors before them, weaving was a household function wherein every homestead became a miniature textile factory. From these homes came linens, clothing, and bedding so fine that

nothing more lovely can be woven on machines today.

Pioneer weaving was adapted from that of colonial times, but because of the migration of many European craftsmen to the West, the weaving arts became a mixture of several cultures and traditions. Though the weaving skills and tools were universal, the varied backgrounds of the people offered a wide variety of forms and patterns in their woven goods. The origins of the oldest patterns are lost in time. Some borrowed from the Indians down through the centuries from Central and South America, and many of these designs can still be seen in the Indian weaving of the Southwest. Tradition meant a great deal in the designs. A pattern was originally probably a symbol with deep meaning, but to us today it seems just a lovely design.

Fine strands of thread—whether wool, cotton, silk, or linen—were used for making cloth. The washed skeins of thread were dyed, if desired. Then they were wound out on a swift, a turning wheel with adjustable diameter. From the swift, the weaver wound several quills—bobbins made of rolled paper—full of thread. (The present popular craft of quilling derives its name from these quills of rolled paper.) Several quills were prepared at a time, then placed one at a time into the shuttle for weaving.

Reduced to the simplest terms, a loom is simply a framework for stretching the warp (lengthwise threads) and dividing it into parts for the insertion of the weft (crosswise threads), sometimes called the woof or filling.

A loom has three main functions: (1) to keep the warp in order and provide tension; (2) to separate the warp to make "sheds" for the shuttle to pass through; and (3) to drive or beat the weft threads together to make a solid web. The more harnesses or heddles (warp holders) a loom has, the more intricate a design can be, since the warp can be separated in many ways.

There are many kinds of looms, from simple wooden frames or stick looms to complicated harness looms. In early days looms set up with a harness of two heddles frames were used for the simplest weaving—plain linen sheets, linsey woolsey, and rag carpeting. These looms were found in many pioneer homes until textile mills were established.

Hand looms were brought across the plains or were made by pioneer woodworkers. Some of the homemade looms were clumsy, and manipulating them was hard and fatiguing. Beautiful weaving could be produced on a crude loom made from a few sticks, but the pioneer women found it more efficient to weave on a loom that did its full share of the work.

In pioneer homes where looms were not available, a simpler form of weaving was practiced, using the backstrap loom, which had been used anciently by the Indians. The name backstrap refers to the way the loom worked: one end was anchored to something stationary and the other was tied to the weaver's waist. Loops of two sticks were used to separate the warp.

Another simple loom used in earlier

times was the stick loom, made of strips or sticks of wood five to six inches long with a hole in the end of each. The warp threads were pulled through the holes; a double thread was usually used, with the length of the thread determined by the length of the article to be woven. The weft threads were simply woven in and out over the sticks, six or eight in number, always starting and ending at the center. As the weaving in and out continued, the woven article was moved backward onto the warp threads by carefully pulling the wooden needles two inches forward, one at a time. The woven strips produced were used for belts, straps, bell pulls, and trimmings or were stitched together in strips to form longer articles, such as rugs or covers for furniture.

A pioneer child learned simple weaving processes on a wooden or cardboard frame loom, a square form with nails or pegs along each of the four sides. The loom was warped with the threads, and then the woof or fiber was interwoven across it. The woven squares produced were used for hot pads, pin cushions, doilies, and pillow covers, and, when sewn together in larger squares, made very warm substantial coverlets and shawls.

Spool weaving delighted many young pioneer girls and was used to produce colorful rounds of woven braid that were sewn together to make chair-seat covers, small floor rugs, and other practical articles. The loom was a spool of wood with four small-headed nails in the top, and yarn, heavy string, or cord was hooked over the nails to form a

stitch. When a woven cord was completed, it was sewn together in rounds. This type of weaving used up small lengths of leftover yarn and was often colorful and sturdy. Young children could do this type of weaving with ease.

Another pioneer loom was called the rigid heddle loom, so called because it had no moving parts. Heddle looms vary in size, from the rigid heddle to larger two- and four-heddle looms. Though they were standard equipment in many pioneer homes, today they are primarily used by weaving enthusiasts. Special books on weaving are available at libraries and bookstores for those who are interested in this type of weaving.

CLOTHING

In spite of good care, patching, and darning, pioneer clothes wore out rapidly with the hard wear they received. When the first struggles to provide food and shelter abated, the pioneers turned their attention to replacing their clothes.

Animal skins provided the first ready materials. Deer and buffalo provided buckskin coats and pants for the men and boys and also moccasins for footwear. With fabrics in short supply, the pioneer mother was hard-pressed to find other suitable materials to clothe herself and her family.

One amusing story was told about a pioneer mother who sent her husband to buy shirts for their boys from California immigrants. He arrived too late to buy the shirts but was able to buy a pair of bed curtains, which he took home to his wife. Since they were quite colorful, with bright red roses and blue flying birds, the boys were indignant and the mother disappointed. Realizing that she couldn't make shirts out of the material, she looked around for something more desirable. A straw tick covered with a material called hickory ticking seemed more appropriate, so she made the shirts out of the ticking and had enough left over to make a dress for her daughter, who later wrote in her journal: "...and I was so proud to wear a dress that had neither rags nor patches." (Mabel Harmer, *Story of the Mormon Pioneers* [Salt Lake City: Deseret Press, 1943], p. 141)

In cases where ticking wasn't available, clothing was made out of wagon covers. These clothes had one essential quality for pioneer use—they were sturdy enough to stand the wear and tear of many seasons.

Patterns

Since necessity was the mother of invention, women learned the art of pattern making, and pioneer seamstresses saved every scrap of paper they could find for that purpose. It is said that one woman, who had been seamstress in England, brought with her a pattern for men's pants, and from that pattern pants were cut for nearly every man in the

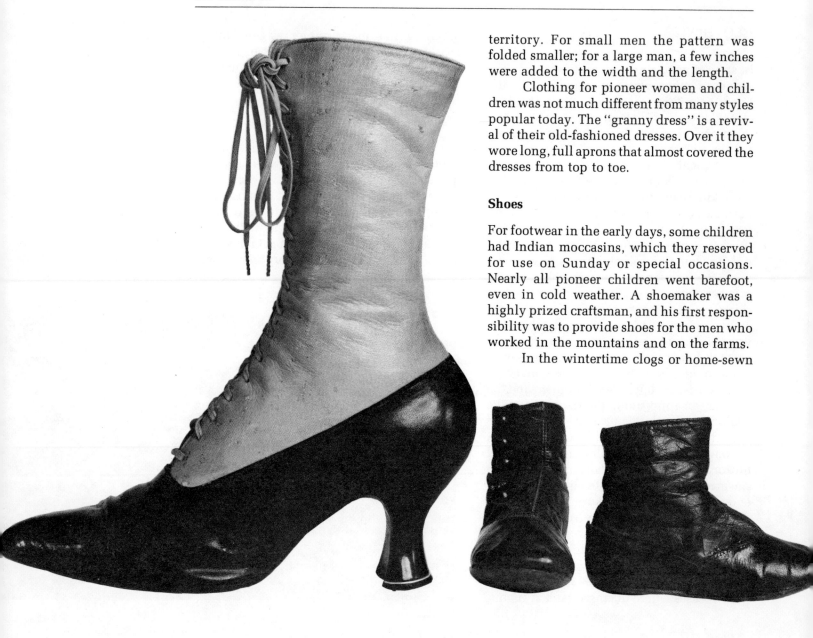

territory. For small men the pattern was folded smaller; for a large man, a few inches were added to the width and the length.

Clothing for pioneer women and children was not much different from many styles popular today. The "granny dress" is a revival of their old-fashioned dresses. Over it they wore long, full aprons that almost covered the dresses from top to toe.

Shoes

For footwear in the early days, some children had Indian moccasins, which they reserved for use on Sunday or special occasions. Nearly all pioneer children went barefoot, even in cold weather. A shoemaker was a highly prized craftsman, and his first responsibility was to provide shoes for the men who worked in the mountains and on the farms.

In the wintertime clogs or home-sewn

cloth shoes were sometimes worn. Shoes made from cottonwood or box elder wood were serviceable but often uncomfortable. Another kind of shoe was made with a leather top and wooden bottom, much like today's popular clogs.

As settlements grew and stock flourished, more leather became available for shoes, and as home tannery processes improved, so did the quality of leather. But preparing hides into leather was a difficult process, so eventually most tanning was done commercially.

Hats

Head coverings were necessary both from a practical standpoint and for aesthetic reasons. Sunbonnets were the first and most familiar head coverings for women. An absolute necessity in the summer, they covered the head and shielded the face from the hot sun and scorching winds. Relatively inexpensive to make, they were usually fashioned of calico or other cotton fabric.

Later on, women's hats were made from heavier cloth, such as denim or percale. Using a pattern, the women cut out and sewed together triangular pieces of material for the crown and added a larger doughnut-shaped piece for the brim. The brim was usually made of double thickness of the material, perhaps with padding between the layers. Quilting or starch were sometimes used to help hold the hats' shape. Often flowers made from "book-muslin" (something like our or-gandy of today) were added for decoration.

Men's hats were generally made from skins or hides of animals, and some of these became the famous "beaver hats."

Straw hats for both men and women came later. Straw grown in the countryside was soaked in warm water to make it more pliable. Then the straws were braided, with seven straws used for work hats and up to eleven for dress hats. The braid was dampened and pressed flat under a heavy weight, then sewn into a hat shape with strong thread. Flax straw was popular, as were oat and wheat straw. Some pioneers raised a special kind of straw called towse straw, which was considered to be more suitable for straw hats because it was coarse, long, hollow, and more pliable.

Straw for hats could be dyed, using the same vegetable dyes that were used for dyeing cloth, or bleached white with sulphur fumes. Colored straw was used for making flowers and trimmings. Horse hair, dyed and braided, was also used to trim hats, adding stiffness to a brim or bonnet. Hats in some settlements took on a distinctive style of shape, so that wherever people from those areas went, they could be identified by their straw hats.

With the coming of the railroad and commerce from the outside, millinery shops were opened where skilled seamstresses provided the discriminating pioneer lady with beautiful bonnets and hats made from velvet and silk, with trimmings such as feathers, flowers, and lace.

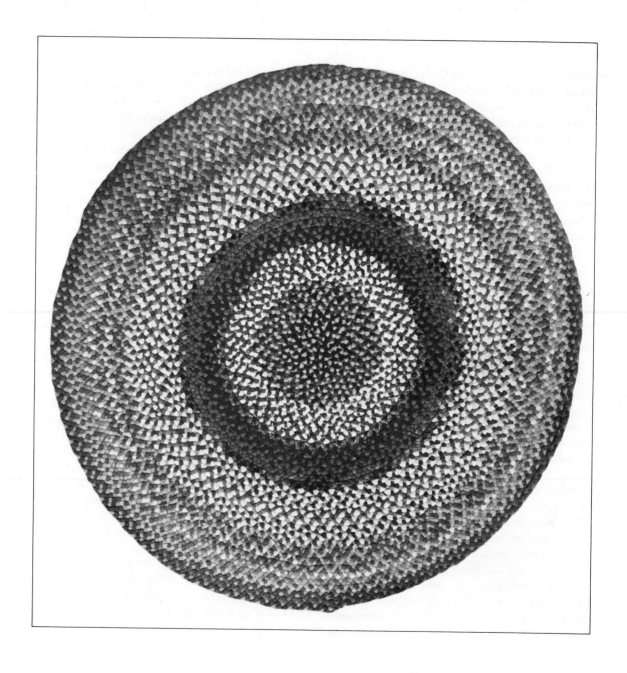

CHAPTER NINE

RUG MAKING

Among the necessary furnishings in the frontier home were floor coverings to provide warmth and comfort and add a note of brightness to the rooms.

The first pioneer homes had hard-packed dirt floors, which were difficult to keep clean, even when they were swept with hemlock brooms or turkey feathers. When dirt floors were replaced with pine or spruce boards, housewives began to make rugs to protect them and add comfort to the home.

The first rugs were made from the skins of animals, hides of deer, buffalo, bear, and, later, the sheep raised on the homestead. The pioneer homemaker knew the age-old art of braiding, hooking, and weaving rugs, and as soon as scraps of fabric became available, she hoarded them to eventually make a rug.

One writer said: "How many operations of bleaching and breaking and boiling these home products had to go through before they came out at last as faultless as the fruits of the eastern looms." (Ellen S. Bowles, *Rug Making* [New York: Little, Brown and Co., 1927], p. 101.)

The Braided Rug

The simplest rug to make was the braided rug, because it could be made with a minimum of equipment. One needed only a supply of suitable fabrics, some strong thread, and a needle, such as a lacing needle or bodkin.

The finished product had many advantages, all of which contributed to its popularity. It was often beautiful as well as long-lasting, fairly easy to make, and just about any kind of woolen material could be used in it. Pioneer rug makers used old suits, overcoats, trousers, shirts, scarves, capes, blankets, and other garments or coverings. The heaviest woolens had the best wearing qualities and were ideal for braiding, but a combination of various woolen materials made a handsome braided rug. Rugs that were well made and well braided from old material often lasted a lifetime. Those with little variation in the two sides could be reversed periodically for longer wear.

Preparations for braiding a rug were the same for our grandmothers as they are for us today. The old garments and materials selected are first washed thoroughly and then all seams are ripped apart and irregular and bulky places such as buttonholes are cut out. To achieve a balanced color scheme, both bright and subdued colors are used, with the arrangement of color planned in advance as far as possible. In pioneer homes most of the materials were on hand when the braiding commenced; however, sometimes the rug was started with a modest amount of material and enlarged or expanded as additional material was collected, resulting in a homey hit-or-miss pattern that gave the rugs individual character.

If the material is to be dyed, the rug maker usually finds it advisable to cable the fabric first. A cable is made by cutting the material in strips, folding each side lengthwise toward the center, folding in half lengthwise again, and sewing the edges to-gether with large blind stitches. Though this takes some time, it makes the actual braiding process faster and more efficient. Thinner material can be filled with less desirable woolen scraps to make all the cables of uniform thickness. The width of the strips used may vary from one and one-half to three or more inches, depending on the thickness of the material. If strips need to be joined together, the ends are cut on the bias and finely sewn together by hand. If there is a difference in the right or wrong side of the material, the best side is kept on top.

After the material is cabled, it is made into skeins about 15 inches long and tied with a piece of twine to hold them together during dyeing. After dyeing, the skeins are hung up to dry, then rolled into balls so they will be neat and easy to use.

In changing colors while braiding, it is helpful to plan the changes at the end of a complete round in the rug for the sake of uniformity. Usually unbraided cabling that is twice the circumference of the rug is sufficient to make one row around. If the strip is too short, a piece of similar material can be joined on. The traditional braided rug has the lighter colors of fabric in the center and darker colors on the outside. Bright colors are alternated with darker colors or neutral tones.

To begin the actual braiding, choose three colors. Sew the ends of two of the cables firmly together on the wrong side so no seam shows. Lap the end of the third cable over the right side of the seam of the other two, with the raw edge tucked in, then baste securely

with a blindstitch. The three cables form a T-shape.

To begin braiding, fold the left cable toward you over the center cable, then fold the right one over. Pull each fold tightly to make a hard, firm braid, with the seam side inside the braid. (The process is exactly the same as that which is used in braiding hair.) The braiding works better if the cables are clamped or weighted to a table, making it possible to pull each fold tightly and firmly.

The oval braided rug was the most popular choice of early rug makers. For a round braided rug, no basic center is required, but a 6' x 8' oval rug calls for a center braid two feet in length; a 9' x 12' rug has a center of three feet.

After the braiding is under way, the rug is laced or sewn together. Lacing is done with the right side up, as is the braiding, and is accomplished by working back and forth from one braid to another by going under each loop between the two edges, skipping none, and drawing the thread very tightly so absolutely no thread is visible between the two loops.

In the round rug, three outside braids are sewn to one inside braid to keep the rug flat. As the rug progresses, less allowance is needed, but on rounded corners, sew two outside braids to one inside braid, to prevent a "cupping" effect in the finished rug. For lacing, use a long sack needle, preferable with a blunt tip so it won't catch the material. The needle should not penetrate the material, but should be laced only through the loop of

braid. Pioneer women often used extra heavy waxed or linen thread, which today is still the best. The use of a double thread is desirable.

When turning at the end of the basic center of an oval rug, lace two outside loops to one inside loop in order to add fullness for a new turn. This double stitching is done three times at the end to keep the braid flat—once just before reaching the end, once at the end, and once just after the end. Thereafter, on the turns, estimate just how many extra loops are needed to make a smooth turn without cupping or fullness. A heavy flatiron on the rug may keep it from slipping.

To end the rug, "pigtail" the last braid on the curve directly across from the point at which the rug started, by trimming the last six to eight inches of each of these cables to a point, and folding and basting them. Braid the pigtail to the end in a slim point, and fasten securely with thread. Tuck the end of the pigtail underneath a cable loop and fasten securely.

Hooked Rugs

Rug hooking is as venerable a craft as rug braiding. Making hooked rugs is a laborious process, because each stitch has to be pulled through a mesh of background fabric, one stitch at a time. The pioneer craftswoman who had patience and time and was adept in the use of her hands could make a beautiful rug from whatever materials she could salvage. As in so many other pioneer crafts, frugality was the mother of invention and the motivating trait of the homemaker. These resourceful women found that rug hooking provided a use for scrap materials too worn or too small for any other purpose. They chose the patterns for the rugs from their everyday lives—flowers, farm animals, churches, barns, patriotic symbols, plants, sun, and storms.

Hooked rugs wear well because of their sturdy backing and thick pile. Hooking is essentially a matter of filling in a backing of meshlike canvas, monk's cloth, or burlap. Our foremothers used homespun, linsey woolsey, linens, and cotton cloth for the foundations of their rugs. Discarded wagon covers were strong and sturdy and made ideal rug backing; the worn places were cut out and only the good parts used. Still later, when burlap or gunny sacks came into use, the housewife washed and pressed them, and used them for their backing material. Lengths of yarn or strips of cut fabrics were hooked, or pushed, through the backing and tied to provide a rich, thick nap. Using different colors in outlined areas gave the pattern shape.

The early hooks were made of wood or bone and were basically shaped like a large crochet hook. Later the rug hooks were made of metal by a blacksmith. The metal hook was then set in a wooden handle to make it easier and more comfortable to use. Still later, a latch was added to keep the yarn from getting tangled

The early hooked rugs were designed by the makers to please themselves. One elderly woman said she saw her grandmother withdraw a charred stick from the fire, drop it in a basin of cold water, and then use it to mark off her design. Later, paper patterns and stencils were used and exchanged with the neighbors and friends.

To prepare the hooking fabric, rags were torn apart, then washed in lukewarm water and suds. If the fabric was to be dyed, homemade dyes were used. After the desired color was set, the material was rinsed well and dried; then the cloth was cut or torn into the short pieces for hooking. If the completed rug was askew, it was blocked by placing a damp towel over it and stretching to the desired shape. It was allowed to dry for 24 hours; then the edges were finished with a blind stitch or a facing.

Woven Rag Rugs

Another popular floor covering in pioneer homes was the woven or rag rug. The warp (lengthwise) thread used in rag rugs needed to be strong and durable. Warp for pioneer carpets was often shipped in, but a limited supply was manufactured locally. The warp thread was usually dyed several colors, resulting in an attractive stripe on the finished product.

Almost any kind of cloth was used for the woof or filling, but woolens weren't mixed with cottons. Worn-out clothing and rags, household linens, and old blankets were most often used. After washing, they were dyed the desired color. Then they were torn into strips ¾ to 1½ inches wide and the strips were sewn together to make a long strand, which was usually wound into a ball. There was a certain knack in sewing carpet rags, and the experienced seamstress knew just how to gauge her work so the cloth was uniform and even.

When the strips of woof were ready, they were wound on shuttles. The loom was then prepared with the warp. Looms used for weaving rugs were heavy to handle and took up much room, but they were sturdy and long-lasting. Threading the loom with the warp involved more careful work than the actual weaving. Twelve threads to an inch was an average number in fine rug making.

When the loom was properly warped and the rags wound on the shuttles, the weaver sat down and, by means of a foot treadle, lifted half the warp up so the shuttle could go across between the two lines of warp. Then the first warp was lowered and the second warp raised and once again the woof was sent through on the shuttle. Each threading of the shuttle was accompanied by a beating by the reed, which was attached to a heavy part of the framework. The weaving process went on hour after hour, day after day, until the carpet was completed.

In days when all the floor coverings in pioneer homes were hand woven, sewing bees were popular. A group of friends and relatives would sit around a large basket of cut rags, where for hours they would sew and wind, their voices keeping time to their needles. Usually lunch would be served, after which the visiting and sewing would con-tinue until the basket of soft, fluffy rags had all been sewn in strips and rolled into big hard balls of carpet rags ready to be woven into rugs.

When the woven carpet was ready to be laid, the rude wooden floor in the home would be thoroughly scrubbed and new straw would be brought from the barnyard and laid smoothly for a pad. Then the men of the family, with the help of the women, would carefully place the carpet over the straw, stretch it, and tack it into place.

A good handmade rug was firm and solid so it would hold together under wear of feet or the pull of a broom, and heavy enough to lie flat on the floor. A light rug that was easily skuffed up was unsightly as well as dangerous. Other important considerations were that the rug should be as handsome in color, design, and texture as possible. Many pioneer rugs filled these requirements beautifully.

All of the oldtime methods of making rugs are still reliable today, and many modern craftswomen create beautiful braided, hooked, and woven rugs for their homes. Often they are used as floor coverings, but some of the most beautifully designed rugs are used as wall hangings.

For the less experienced woman who is not inclined to design her own rug, a wide variety of preplanned and prepared kits are available in craft stores or catalogs. Using these kits, a woman has the pleasure of making something for her home with the skillful use of her hands.

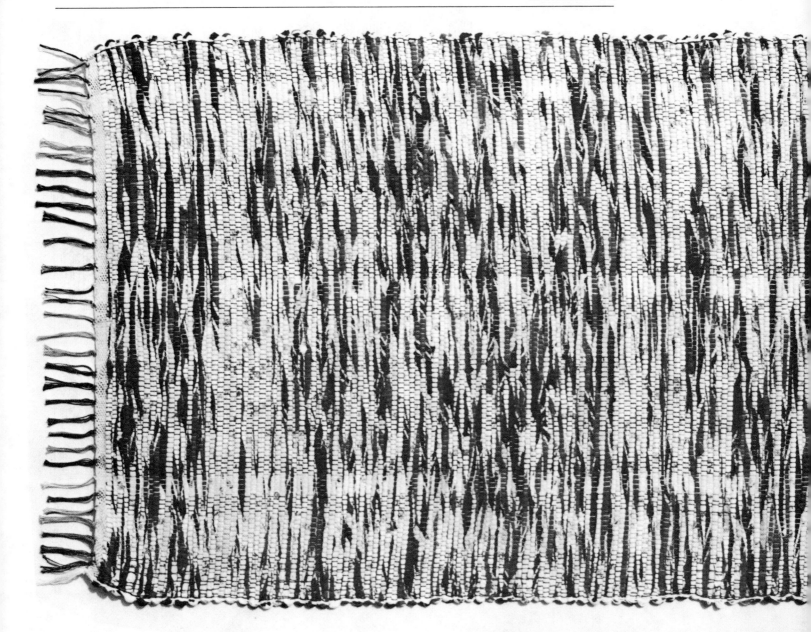

CHAPTER TEN

SOAP MAKING

In order to keep her family and her household clean, the energetic pioneer housewife had to make her own soap. For months, she would save every bit of leftover fat and grease. Bacon rinds, trimmings from meat, and other scraps of fat were stored away in a huge crock to wait for soapmaking time. When enough fat had accumulated it was melted down in a large kettle and either allowed to settle, the fat rising to the top and the sediment falling to the bottom, or clarified by straining the sediment out.

The fat was combined with lye to produce soap. Concentrated lye for soapmaking was unknown in pioneer times, but the pioneers made a good substitute. All winter they saved white ashes from the fireplace (ashes from maple, cottonwood, hickory or corncobs were the most desirable). These were put into a leach hopper, a container made from half a hollow log with slanting board ends. The hopper was set on an incline, and water was poured over the ashes and allowed to drip slowly through them, dissolving and absorbing the lye in the ashes. After repeated stirrings and skimmings, the ashes settled to the bottom, and the lye water was ready. The lye was collected in a bucket as it was poured from the lowered end of the hopper. It was then put into a large kettle and over a fire in the yard, and the grease was added to it. As the mixture heated, the lye broke down the grease, and after cooking slowly for several hours, a thick soap syrup was formed.

To test the mixture, a sample was taken frequently in a spoon and cooled in a saucer.

The experienced soap maker could tell if the soap was ready from the way it "set up" in the saucer. She would test it with plain water and then with lye water—when a spoonful became firm and white, it was done. The soap was poured carefully into tubs to stand overnight and cool. Some tubfuls were perfumed with fresh mint or other fragrant herbs to be used for hand soap. In the morning, the soap was congealed and firm and ready to be cut into bars, which were allowed to dry until used.

Soft soap was made from lye and grease that didn't cook as long or solidify as firmly as the bar soap. In many pioneer homes, a broken cup or other small pretty container was partially filled with soft soap and placed by the wash basin. The soap was dipped up with two fingers and rubbed over the hands. One pioneer journal notes the soft soap "would start the dirt all right but was very severe when applied to chapped feet which most of the children had, for they went barefooted half of the year and some of them all the year round." (Kate B. Carter, comp., *Treasures of Pioneer History*, 1956, vol. 5, p. 183.)

Homemade lye water was used for all-purpose cleaning, as well as for removing hulls from corn to prepare it for "hulled corn" or hominy. In many pioneer homes, soap was much too precious to be used for cleaning floors; sand was used instead where it was available. Clean sand was sprinkled over the floor, then swept off.

Another cleaning agent was introduced to the pioneer woman by the Indians. This soap substitute came from the yucca plant native to the West and was called the "ooze plant" by the Indians. When its large tap root was crushed, it produced a foamy lather that quickly removed dirt. The pioneers found this soap excellent for woolens, silks, laces, and other fragile articles, since the lather did not fade delicate colors or shrink wool.

Modern Soapmaking

Today's homemaker can follow in her grandmother's footsteps by making her own soap, but she can forget the boiling and long hours of work. Soapmaking at home is still an excellent way to salvage waste fat and grease, using the convenient commercial lye found in many grocery stores.

To make soap at home, begin by saving animal fats, such as rancid butter, bacon grease, roast drippings—any animal fats are suitable. Hard soaps can also be made by using vegetable fats, such as shortening, olive oil, castor oil, and coconut oil. Prepare the fat by placing it in a pan and covering it with enough water to settle the sediment. Bring water and fat to a boil, then let them cool. Lift off the clean fat to use for soap. Discard the sediment.

Soap made at home is generally of better quality than that which is purchased, because the glycerin is removed from the fat in the commercial product and sold for other purposes. Homemade soap is a pleasure to use because it has that special quality found in things you make yourself with care and joy.

Homemade soaps can also be used successfully in the modern washing machine if water softener is added to the water.

Making soap requires some patience and can be messy, but practice will improve your product as you learn the techniques and processes involved. A good quality soap can be made by mixing lye and fat at a temperature between 80° and 110° F. Stir the soap mixture constantly until it thickens and begins to form soap. (It should be about the consistency of thick pea soup.) Then pour it into prepared molds until it hardens to shape. Keep it away from drafts while it is hardening.

Equipment necessary for soapmaking:

1. An enamel, earthenware, granite, or stainless steel container, six quarts or larger in size. Lye will corrode such metals as tin or aluminum as well as teflon-coated utensils.

2. Long-handled wooden spoons or a stick to stir the soap.

3. Fine sieve or cheesecloth through which to strain fat.

4. Thermometer to check the temperature of the fat and the lye. A good meat or candy thermometer will do if it has a range from 50° to 270° F.

5. Rubber gloves and apron for safety, since lye can burn the skin.

6. Newspaper or plastic to protect work surfaces.

7. Cardboard boxes, milk cartons, or enamel or glass molds to pour the soap into. These should be lined with wax paper, foil, or a damp cloth. Plastic garbage bags cut open make good liners.

Some precautions to take in making soap are:

1. Don't stand over the lye solution. The fumes rise and may be irritating if inhaled. Turn the eyes and face away from the solution when pouring.

2. Protect hands and work surfaces.

3. Keep lye away from children; it can be fatal if swallowed, and it also burns. Keep an open bottle of vinegar handy to use as a neutralizer for lye burns while you are working. If lye touches skin, wash it off with cold water immediately.

4. When bars of soap are made, if any liquid drops out of the soap, discard it all. There may be undissolved lye present. A good batch of soap will not have pockets in it for undissolved lye.

RECIPES FOR HOMEMADE SOAP

Bar Soap

1 13-ounce can lye
6 cups cold water
5½ pounds clean fat, melted and cooled to
    110° F. (part lard and part coconut or
    cottonseed oil; oils give a finer product,
    and lard is needed for a firm bar)
1 to 2 tablespoons fragrant oils (oil of lemon
    or sassafras)
Food coloring (optional)

In a 2-quart heat-proof bowl, slowly pour lye into cold water and stir with a slotted wooden spoon until dissolved. Cool to 80° F. Put melted fat (at 110° F.) into a 6-quart heat-proof bowl and slowly add lye solution, stirring until well mixed and as thick as honey. Add the perfumed oils and food coloring, but do not stir longer than necessary or mixture will begin to separate. Pour into wooden molds or pasteboard boxes lined with brown paper. Let stand in warm place until firm. Cut into cakes with string or wire. Pile bars on wire racks so air circulates around each cake.

Granulated Soap

10 cups melted, strained fat
10 cups cold water
1 13-ounce can lye
2 tablespoons borax
2 tablespoons ammonia

Measure water into enamel pan or crock. Add lye and stir vigorously until dissolved. Gradually pour the warm fat into the lukewarm lye water, stirring slowly. Dissolve the borax and ammonia in ¼ cup warm water and add to lye. Continue stirring for seven minutes. Cover with an old rug or blanket to keep it warm. Stir occasionally and it will break into granules. Let age two weeks before using.

Oatmeal Soap

1 13-ounce can lye
½ cup ammonia

½ cup powdered borax
2 ounces lanolin (hydrus)
4 teaspoons aromatic oil (rose, etc.)
3 tablespoons ground oatmeal
11 cups melted, strained fat
5 cups soft water or rain water
⅓ cup sugar
3 ounces glycerin

Measure water into crock or enamel pan. Stir vigorously, adding to it, one at a time until dissolved, lye, ammonia, borax, and sugar. Continue stirring until cool. Slowly pour in fat, stirring constantly. Add fragrance and stir 15 minutes. Add lanolin, glycerin, and oatmeal while stirring. By this time the mixture should be thick and creamy. Pour into mold (a glass baking dish lined with wax paper is good). Let stand until firm. Cut into bars, wrap in wax paper, and let stand a week before using.

The following recipes are for a gentle and refined hand soap. They use castor oil or shortening, and both are exceptionally mild and soothing, having a rich lather.

Castor Oil Soap

1½ cups lye
4 cups water
1 cup castor oil
2¾ cups olive oil
2¾ cups coconut oil
2 pounds lard

All-Vegetable Soap

1⅓ cups lye
4 cups water
5½ cups olive oil
2 cups coconut oil
3 cups vegetable shortening

Prepare molds and line them. Measure lye and add to water. Stir solution with wooden spoon to dissolve lye. Measure fat into soap kettle, cutting into chunks. Add oils. Place kettle on low heat and heat as slowly as possible to melt fat. When temperature is between 95° and 98° F., fat should be melted. Remove from heat and stir occasionally to distribute the heat. When fat is melted, add lye mixture, which has also been heated to 95° F. in hot water. (Work on a countertop or table, not the stove.) Keep fats in motion by stirring constantly while lye is added. Lye mix should be poured in a steady, even stream. An old enamel pot makes a good container for lye and water solution. When mixture thickens, which may take from 30 to 90 minutes, it can be poured into molds. If a scent is desired, add it to the soap before pouring into molds. Cover molds as soon as they are filled. Let cool for at least 24 hours before removing from molds.

Soap may be shaped into bars and aged in open air for two weeks before using. If there is a powdery layer of soap ash on top, it may be scraped off. If the soap is soft, it may be molded into little balls or carved into decorative shapes.

CHAPTER ELEVEN

CANDLE MAKING

Other than fire lights, for a long time the only lighting inside log cabins came from "ketches." These were an old-world type of candle made from melted animal suet, for which the tallow was usually plentiful. These tallow candles gave a feeble, sputtering light, smoked badly, and were often bad-smelling and dirty.

Then, as now, candles were made in tin molds with small wicks of cotton or linen strung through the molds, which were then filled with the melted tallow. After the wax or tallow cooled, the candles were carefully taken out of the mold, trimmed, and frugally used for light. If no molds were available, the candles could be dipped, like the popular bayberry candles found in New England.

As supplies became more available and the pioneer homemaker became more knowledgeable, wax candles similar to the New England bayberry candles were made from berries or pine needles. These candles took a great deal of time and effort but were superior to the tallow candles in many ways.

It would often take as long as twelve hours to pick a ten-quart pail of bayberries. The berries were then picked over and as many leaves and twigs removed as possible. The berries were placed in iron kettles over a fireplace or an outdoor campfire, covered with cold water, and stirred with wooden paddles. The floating debris was skimmed off before the heating began. As the water warmed, the wax rendered from the berries floated to the surface. This process took three or more hours.

The wax solidified as the water cooled. It was skimmed from the water, melted again in hot water in a smaller kettle, and finally strained through several thicknesses of cloth to remove the last bits of foreign matter. The wax was then ready for dipping. This was accomplished by tying wicks of proper lengths to the end of a stick and dipping them over and over into a container of melted wax. The dipping was done quickly and the wax allowed to harden after each dip. At least twenty-four hours were needed to make a candle.

Many households had candle molds, which were helpful in making candles of uniform size, eliminated the tedious task of dipping and speeded up the candlemaking process.

MODERN CANDLEMAKING

Surprisingly, candlemaking is not a difficult craft. It requires a small investment in time and materials, but the finished product can look professional and be a work of art. Instructions for candlemaking follow.

Materials needed

1. Candle mold of cardboard, glass, metal, or waxed carton. Empty milk cartons, glass jars, tin cans, and novel shaped cartons are all suitable. Many commercial molds are now available in craft supply stores.

2. A length of candle wick, gas lamp wick, or waxed string. An old candle may be used to provide the wick for a new candle.

3. Small bolt, nut, or nail to provide a weight to hold the wick straight.

4. Pencil or paper straw from which to suspend the wick.

5. Paraffin, melted wax, or commercial candle wax.

6. Pan or container for melting wax.

7. Old crayons or commercial dyes for coloring wax.

8. Thermometer, such as a candy thermometer with a reading of at least 200° F. A good pouring temperature for hard wax is about 165° F.

Instructions

For the best results, buy refined wax in a slab. Hard wax with a melting point of 140° to 150° F. is used for most candles and is easily obtainable from a craft shop. While ordinary household paraffin can be used, it is not highly recommended because its melting point is too low and it is difficult to remove from molds.

Cut wax into small- to medium-sized chunks and melt in a double-boiler or in a discardable tin can. Do not place the melting pot directly over heat; always heat over hot water. Two pounds of wax equals one quart of liquid, and eight pounds of wax makes a gallon of liquid.

Someone has said, "To pick a wick is a neat trick," and this is true, since a wick that

works for one kind of candle may not be satisfactory for another. A general rule is that the larger the candle is in diameter, the larger the wick should be. String can be used but it burns quickly and leaves a small hole in the center of the candle. Some molds can have a small hole bored in the bottom for the wick, which is knotted and then fastened at the top to a pencil or stick anchor. The bottom of the wick can also be tied to a small nail, nut, or bolt and the top fastened to a pencil placed over the top of the mold. Small metal discs to secure a wick are available.

Creating with color is fun and easy to do. Color rosettes and powdered pigment are available at craft shops. Wax crayons are an inexpensive means of coloring wax, but many authorities say that certain chemicals in the crayons affect the burning qualities of candles and cause smoking and sputtering. Candle perfumes and hardening agents are also available. The coloring agent should be melted with the wax or paraffin until both are completely melted (between 150° and 165° F.)

Many items around the house may be used for molds—milk and ice cream cartons, juice cans of all sizes, plastic and glass containers, and plastic liquid soap bottles. Molds may be preheated and coated lightly inside with oil, but this is not necessary for all molds. If perfumed candles are desired, the scent should be added to the liquid before it is poured into the mold.

While handling hot wax, place molds on a paper to avoid a lot of cleaning up. Pour melted wax slowly, forming a ½-inch-deep layer in the bottom of the mold and allowing it to set for a couple of minutes until the wick is firmly held in place. There is less shrinkage if the wax is allowed to cool before pouring and is poured in small amounts. Continue pouring carefully to eliminate air bubbles until wax is within ½ inch of the top of the mold or desired height. Be sure to save about one cup of wax to fill depressed center resulting from shrinkage as wax cools.

Place the filled mold in the refrigerator to hasten the hardening process. The total cooling time varies with the size of the mold and amount of wax used. When the wax near the wick has settled into a well-shaped hole and hardened, the candle should be firm. Fill the hole with leftover wax and allow to harden. Then let candles dry at least 12 hours.

When candles are dry, cut off the knot from the bottom of the mold and slip the candle out of the mold. If it doesn't come out easily, place it in the refrigerator about two hours. If it still sticks, immerse mold in hot water, then put in refrigerator. Soap bottle molds must be cut away very carefully with a razor blade. To clean wax from containers, heat over very low heat and wipe with paper towel, then wash in hot soapy water.

Many materials may be used for decorating and trimming basic candles. Don't be afraid to try something new. Candlemaking is an enjoyable and fascinating hobby, and candles make excellent gifts. Following are some delightful variations of the plain candle that our grandparents used.

LAYERED CANDLE. This is made by pouring a small amount of colored paraffin into a mold, allowing it to harden, then adding more paraffin in another color. Let each layer harden before adding a new color. To achieve a muted color transition or a subdued color in layered candles, dip the entire candle into uncolored melted paraffin; then coat it by holding the wick and twirling the candle with a steady, even motion.

NOVELTY MOLDS and CARVED CANDLES. Molds can be used to make interesting shapes, such as fruits, vegetables, and animals. They may be decorated with flower petals, leaves, berries, or other shapes by forming these shapes from softened wax. A sharp knife may be used to carve the wax. Holidays and special events may furnish motifs.

BASED CANDLES. This unusual effect is achieved by pouring melted wax or paraffin into an aluminum pie tin, setting a finished, hardened candle upright in the center of the pie tin, and quickly immersing the pie tin in cold water. Be sure to hold the tin in an even, upright position, and be careful not to wet the wick, but to immerse the paraffin completely. Leave the candle in cold water until the base wax curls delicately around center candle in fragile, translucent forms.

CHUNK CANDLE. Put bits of hardened wax into a candle mold before pouring in the melted wax, or press chunks of wax into the top of a partially hardened candle. To make the chunks, pour melted wax onto an un-

greased sheet or large plate; as the wax begins to harden, cut it into chunks.

ROLLED CANDLES. Pour wax out flat into rectangle, lay the wick at one end, and roll the semi-hardened wax around the wick to the other end of the wax. The wax should be pliable enough to roll without cracking.

MOSAIC CANDLES. These are made with the rolling technique. Cut out pieces of soft wax in desired design, lift them carefully, and roll them around the hard base of another candle. It is best to have the design all worked out ahead of time, especially if you are working with several colors. Placing the sheet of poured wax on top of a warm oven or stove top (be sure the burners are off) will help if the wax hardens too quickly.

TEXTURED CANDLES. A rock-like effect can be achieved by dripping water into the mold while the wax or paraffin is still melted. Be careful not to wet the wick, but let water drip around the edges to make irregularly shaped holes in the sides. Crushed ice or ice cubes added to the mold before pouring wax creates unique and interesting textures.

SAND CANDLES. These popular candles can be made on the beach, in a sandbox, or in a sand-filled tub or container. Moisten the sand slightly and scoop out the shape you want. Dig a small hole in the bottom of the sand mold and insert a wick. The sand candle can be any size or shape you want, but if it has legs on it, be sure the legs are all the same depth and size so it will stand evenly and not tip.

CHAPTER TWELVE

DRIED AND WAXED FLOWERS AND FRUITS

During the desolate winter months the pioneer woman longed for a touch of brightness in her home, so she sought ways of capturing a part of summer's brightness or fall's brilliant color. She gathered flowers, weeds, and grasses from the woods, fields, and desert and learned how to dry, press, or duplicate them so she could retain a hint of the gay colors or sweet fragrance during the long winter.

At first the pioneer artist depended on her imagination and used whatever materials were handy. But as settlements grew, persons who had special skills or methods in artwork offered courses of instruction. In these art classes women learned to make flowers of wool, paper, wax, hair, and other materials.

One pioneer diary tells of a course of instruction for making wax fruits. It cost $6.00 and was taught by a lady who was excellent in the craft. That was a considerable amount of money for those days, but one undaunted girl did a family's wash for 50¢ a week until she had earned enough money to attend the class. There she learned to make wax fruit, a cherished decoration in the parlor of the pioneer home, and to arrange waxed fruit, flowers made from silk, wool, and hair, or natural dried flowers in colorful splendor beneath a glass dome. These decorative arrangements were placed in prominent places, usually in the center of a table or on a whatnot shelf. One such dome contained a beautiful bouquet of natural grasses, grains, and flowers arranged in a lovely vase. In this bouquet some of the grasses were dyed green with vegetable dyes and others were frosted with alum; all were arranged artistically with tinted flowers.

Another arrangement of wax fruit under a dome was brought across the plains in a covered wagon in 1861. One that was made in 1855 contained a beautiful wax cross with white flowers on it. Still another had flowers of cloth, delicately tinted, with a fancy bird and a number of yellow and black butterflies.

Flowers made of wool were often framed or boxed in lovely grained wood, as were hair flowers. One lovely wreath was made from the hair of the wives and daughters of Brigham Young; preserved in an oval-shaped frame of oak, it can still be seen in the Lion House in Salt Lake City.

The delicacy of many kinds of flowers, including roses and wild flowers, was re-created in cornhusks. The husks were cleaned, bleached, boiled in vegetable dyes, and then fashioned into long-lasting flowers to grace a table or picture frame. Directions for making the roses are as follows:

Using damp and pliable husks that have been soaked in water, cut six or seven of the base ends into two-inch lengths. Bind them together to form a flower center. Make several centers at the same time while husks are damp. Next, cut small, medium, and large petals from the husks. Dry these on a flat surface, then curl the upper ends by rolling them over a small stick or pencil. Gather the pointed ends of the petals and fasten them to the centers. Add as many petals as needed for the size of the rose desired. When the flowers are finished, fasten lengths of slender sticks or wires to the blossoms to make the stems.

Cornhusk butterflies and birds were also fashioned out of pliable husks. The wings of the insects were made by cutting and pleating husks in the shape of wings, then inserting the wings into a wooden clothespin, which formed the body. The wings were cut while damp and then pressed dry.

The following instructions for making wax fruit, which are still applicable today, were written in a pioneer journal in 1869.

Materials: Well formed fruit for pattern, plaster paris, white wax, cardboard, white covered wires, paints.

Selection of fruit suitable: Apricot, apples, orange, lemon, lime, pears, cherries, plum (green gage, and blue plum), grapes (white and dark), currants (red and white), strawberries, raspberries, raisins, peaches, tomatoes and watermelon.

Method: Make a box from the cardboard that will give good depth and width for the fruit you desire to mold. For example, a pear will require a deep box. Mix the plaster of paris with water and pour the mix into the box to a depth sufficient to cover one half the fruit you are molding. Taking the pear, for example, you lay the pear in the mix so that exactly one-half is above and one-half buried in the mix. Allow this to set. Remove the pear and with a sharp knife smooth the entire plaster surface. Cut a hole on each side of the mold. This makes half of a mold.

Grease the entire surface and the mold of the fruit, or pear. Replace the fruit and pour the plaster paris mix over it until it is well covered. When this has set, tear the cardboard away. The mold will break apart from the greased surface, making two perfect half molds. Now remove the pear and make sure the molds are well greased.

Pour the melted white wax into the lower half mold, place the upper half and fasten securely by the holes on each side. While the wax is hot shake the mold to keep the wax in motion. Allow sufficient time for the wax to cool and set. Unfasten the upper half from the lower half and carefully remove the fruit from the mold. If small holes or uneven surface appears the wax must be remelted and the operation repeated until you have a perfect specimen.

To finish the fruit tint with paints to resemble the natural fruit. For the pear take the stem from the original fruit and fasten it to the waxed one. The apricot, orange, lemon and lime are tinted with burnt umber. The apricot is sometimes made showing the two halves. To do this a wax mold must be made of the stone and then paint the stone and place it in the half apricot. For this type of fruit the paint is mixed in the hot wax and poured into the mold together.

For fruit such as cherries, grapes, currants and raisins make a cardboard box long enough to hold several at one operation. The stem for this type of fruit is made from wire and the fruit placed on to resemble the natural clusters. The cherry stem may be used like the pear and apple is used. The raisin is quite simple to make. Press a raisin or several of them into the plaster paris mix just half way down. Allow this to set and remove. Grease the molds well and pour melted resin into them. When this sets the raisin is complete. The watermelon is painted after removing the mold. The seeds from the natural fruit are set into the wax to appear realistic.

A basket container is made from the covered wire and well waxed. It should have a handle so that the clusters of fruit may be fastened securely. The fruit is placed in an attractive manner in the basket and the whole is covered with a glass globe which stands on a round wooden base. (Norma H. Morris, in *Heart Throbs of the West*, vol. 2, pp. 474-75.)

Pressed Flowers

Usually the flowers were dried by pressing them in a book between sheets of paper with a weight placed on top. Simple flowers such as pansies—flowers that lay flat and were not bulky—and ferns were the easiest to press without removing the stem and foliage.

Only flowers at the peak of blossom color were pressed. Bruised or faded blossoms were discarded. The flowers were best picked after the dew had evaporated or in dry weather, and they retained their beauty better if they were pressed within half an hour after picking. Very delicate flowers were pressed whole, while large flowers were taken apart and pressed petal by petal. Pressing flowers in books took three to four weeks. The variety of ways to use them was limited only by the

imagination of the artist arranging them.

Wild flowers and weeds found in meadows and nearby hills provided ideal materials for pressed flower compositions. Heather, wheat, baby's breath, Queen Anne's lace, grasses, ferns, thistles, wood roses, flowering weeds, and pods of all kinds found their way into old-fashioned bouquets and picture frames, in casual clusters or arranged in delicate patterns.

Air-Dried Flowers

The simplest way of drying, however, was to let the air do it. This method worked well with ferns, grasses, wild goldenrod, and plants with tiny heads of blossoms, such as strawflowers and larkspur. The leaves were stripped off and the flowers tied in a loose bunch with string. The bunches were then hung upside down in a cool, dark, airy place—usually the attic, since the cellar was too damp. Most grasses, grains, shrubs, and branches were dried upright in a container. Drying time was one to two weeks, depending on the size of the flowers and the humidity. Grasses and flowers dried in the sun faded to a soft natural beige and then were mixed with colored dry flowers to give accent. Sometimes they were tinted soft shades with vegetable dyes. Bamboo, marsh grass, pussy willows, autumn leaves, and berries were used to outline and as backdrop for arrangements. Some of the larger branches were dried in gentle curves that added a softness to the arrangement.

Sand-Dried Flowers

Another method of preserving the color and form of flowers was sand drying. Surprisingly, the sand around the Great Salt Lake was found to be among the best in the world for drying and preserving flowers.

The sand was washed and strained to eliminate debris and then dried in the sun for two to three days. The following pioneer method for drying flowers is the same process used today by florists and artists who dry flowers commercially.

1. Place at least one inch of sand as a base in a box or container. If the flower is fragile and needs a support, use a notched piece of cardboard to hold the flower head.

2. Using a small pitcher with a pouring spout, gently pour sand in the corners and large areas of the container.

3. Sift sand gently around the flower by using a fine spray from the clenched fist. Completely cover the flower with sand.

4. Leave the flower in sand for at least two weeks for thorough drying. A lid is not necessary.

5. When the flower is dry, carefully tilt the container and gently pour the sand out, being sure to always pour in the same direction and never reversing the movement of sand.

Potpourri

One of the pleasantest occupations of the pioneer woman was the preparation of potpourri, a fragrant flower and herb mixture that was stirred whenever the air in poorly ventilated rooms needed freshening or was kept in cupboards and closets to scent linens and clothing.

There were two methods of making potpourri—a moist method and a dry method. The dry method was less complicated than the quicker moist method and allowed the flowers to retain their color. In the early morning hours, after the dew had disappeared, the pioneer woman selected newly opened roses and other flowers from her garden. She removed the petals from the blossoms and spread them to dry on a screen or taut cheesecloth. Then she put them in a warm, dry, sunless place, such as an attic, where the air circulated around them. The drying process often took ten days or more.

Sometimes the petals were gathered and dried throughout the summer, and made into a potpourri in the fall. The dried petals were stored in airtight containers in a dark place until ready to be used. Usually the various flowers were kept in separate containers and labeled for easy indentification.

In making potpourri, dried petals were mixed with the other ingredients—aromatic dried leaves, spices, fragrant oils. The mixture was allowed to mellow for about six

weeks in a tightly sealed container in a dark spot, then placed in cloth bags or rose jars. The fragrance captured in the jars penetrated and freshened rooms for many years. An occasional shaking or stirring renewed the scent.

Although recipes for making potpourri were passed along from one neighbor to another, the individualistic nature of the women led them to improvise and add their own touches in mixing and blending fragrances. They experimented with flowers, herbs, and spices in their own kitchens and gardens, letting their noses be the guides in preparing just the right blend. Unlike recipes used in cooking, potpourri recipes were not spoiled by changing quantities or by adding another scent as a personal preference. Here are some of the favorite recipes.

Dry Potpourri

In a large bowl mix about ½ cup orrisroot (powder or granules) to 1 quart dried rose petals and tiny buds. Seal and allow to set for three weeks, stirring contents every other day. Add to rose petal and orrisroot mixture the following: ½ cup patchouli, ¼ cup sandalwood chips, ½ cup vetiver, 2 teaspoons frankincense and myrrh mixed, 1 teaspoon crushed gum benzoin, 1 teaspoon cinnamon, 1 teaspoon crushed cloves, and 1 tablespoon slivered orange peel. Mix thoroughly with a wooden spoon. Add 10 drops rose oil for extra fragrance. Place in a jar and seal for one month. (Be sure to keep out of direct light if you use a glass jar.) Then stir with a wooden spoon and put into individual containers.

Potpourri Delight

2 quarts dried rose and other garden flower petals
½ pint dried lemon verbena leaves
2 tablespoons dried lavender flowers
2 tablespoons mixed dried herbs (basil, marjoram, bay leaf, rosemary)
2 tablespoons mixed spices (ginger, nutmeg, cinnamon)
5 crushed cloves
½ vanilla bean, crushed
2 tablespoons grated citrus rind
4 tablespoons orrisroot
5 drops essential oil

Mix the dried flower petals and leaves in a bowl. Add a mixture of the herbs, spices, cloves, vanilla bean, citrus rind, and orrisroot. Blend gently and add oil. Store for 6 weeks, then put into rose jars.

Moist Rose Potpourri

2 quarts rose petals (fresh fragrant varieties—pick in the morning)
Coarse salt (kosher type—do not use iodized salt)
2 ounces orris powder
¼ ounce ground mace
¼ ounce ground cloves
1 small stick cinnamon (crushed)
¼ ounce ground nutmeg

¼ ounce ground *allspice*
5 drops *oil of rose or oil of jasmine*

Gather freshly opened, unbruised petals in a variety of colors. Spread out on paper toweling and let dry until they lose about half their bulk and have a leathery (half-dry) look. Place in large jars or crocks with lids, layering roses with salt. Continue alternating layers of roses and salt, ending with salt, until container is just two-thirds full. Cover tightly and store away from heat and light for three weeks. (If a liquid forms, press down petals with the back of a spoon and pour off residual liquid.) After three weeks, remove from jars. Shake away salt. If petals have caked together, flake lightly with fingers. Place petals in a large bowl. Mix orris and the spices together separately and add to roses. Return to jars with tight-fitting lids. Store unopened for six weeks. When ready to use, add oil gradually, stirring gently.

Country Herb Potpourri

¼ cup dried *lemon peel*
¼ cup dried *orange peel*
¼ cup dried *lime peel*
1 cup *marjoram*
1½ cups leaf *rosemary*
½ cup leaf *sage*
1 or 2 bay leaves, *coarsely broken*
¼ cup summer *savory*
1 cup coarse *salt*

To prepare the peels, pare fruits with a vegetable parer; try not to pick up the white pith.

Spread strips of peel on a plate to dry thoroughly. Break them up coarsely; then measure out desired amounts. (The bright yellow, orange, and green peels will add color to potpourri, in addition to a citrus scent.) Blend the herbs and peels together in a big bowl. Mix with hands or wooden spoons, and crush the herbs slightly. Add salt, and mix thoroughly. Let ripen in jars with tight-fitting lids, away from light and heat, for four to six weeks; then place in a decorative jar with a tight-fitting lid. When ready to use, open jar, stir potpourri gently, and leave the cover off for a while. Replace cover tightly when not in use, to prolong the life of the fragrances. This mixture has a refreshing citrus-herbal fragrance. If you want a stronger citrus scent, you may increase the amount of peel.

Spice Potpourri

1 tablespoon anise seed, *crushed*
1 teaspoon whole allspice, *crushed*
5 or 6 nutmegs, *coarsely broken*
2 cup whole *cloves*
½ teaspoon ground *cinnamon*
2 or 3 whole vanilla beans, *cut or broken into small pieces*
1 cup coarse *salt*

Crush the anise seed and allspice, preferably with a mortar and pestle. Break the nutmegs with a hammer or other heavy object. Mix all the spices carefully together. Add salt, and blend well. Ripen and store.

CHAPTER THIRTEEN

TOYS AND DOLLS

Pioneer children, like children of all ages, managed to make their own fun. They rolled and dried their own clay marbles and in stormy weather dug holes in the dirt floor of the house to roll them in—mother hurrying to fill the rings up again and pat them down after the game was over.

They drew checkerboards on pieces of wood with charcoal and used colored buttons or stones as men. The same board could be cleaned off and a game of tic-tac-toe drawn on again with the charcoal. A Christmas journal also tells of a young boy receiving a "corn hoop" made by an older brother. He spent many happy hours rolling it with the help of a stick.

Out of a need for entertainment and with the materials at hand, some delightful toys were made. Many pioneer toys were made from the simplest materials and patterns, but their naive charm is still appealing to children today. Balls, game boards, doll furniture, pull toys, puzzles, whirligigs, and other toys have not lost their charm through the years.

Stuffed animals, made of scraps of patchwork sewn together, were favorites and the patterns were original, often resembling stylized or imaginative shapes of animals with little concern for accurate proportions. Many of these stuffed animals, such as cats, dogs, and rabbits, were two-dimensional. Sometimes they were stuffed with balsam needles and used as door stops when not in play.

The soft, stuffed clutch ball was another

favorite toy. Sewn out of pieces of cloth in a variety of colors, it was stuffed with whatever was at hand, including wool, scraps of cotton, sawdust, and pine needles. Soft balls were also crocheted or knitted out of scraps of yarn and then stuffed. Sometimes they were lined with muslin or cotton to hold the stuffing inside.

A favorite toy for little boys was the stick horse or the hobby horse. Imaginative children could make fine steeds out of any old stick; when a head was added with a crosspiece of wood, it became a handsome horse indeed. An old sock stuffed for firmness was sometimes tied on the stick for a head, embellished by a yarn mane, button eyes, and reins made from string or rawhide. These horses gave many hours of happy riding to their owners.

One possession that most pioneer boys cherished was a slingshot. Though it was a favorite toy, at times it was also a practical article, since it could be used for killing small game animals and birds to supply desperately needed food. One journal tells of a young hunter bagging 22 rabbits, 77 squirrels, and 5 pheasants with his slingshot. Made from a Y-shaped branch, the slingshot was put together with heavy twine and a small leather pouch.

Another sling of the David and Goliath type consisted of a piece of leather tied to two cords. This sling was held in one hand and whirled overhead, with one cord released to send a stone sailing from the pouch. Sometimes clay-baked pellets were used for am-

munition. The sling was a simple but effective tool for many years, and even today many young boys love to carry them in their pockets to practice target shooting.

Bean bags were used by pioneer children for a variety of games. They were made of sturdy fabric and sewn together in a variety of patterns, including fish, owls, and turtles. In the early days beans were much too precious to use for filling the bags, so the first bean bags were filled with sawdust, fine gravel, pine needles, or coarse sand.

Since wood was more plentiful than many other materials, skillful, loving fathers carved or pieced together many delightful toys. Usually a soft wood such as pine was used. The toys were sturdily made, and some lasted a lifetime or more, providing joy to pioneer children, their children, and their children's children. Samples of carefully constructed dolls, doll furniture, horses, animals, pull toys, spinning tops, and other articles have been preserved and cherished through the years.

Wooden board games were favorites of children and adults alike. Squares of wood were divided into patterns by carving or drilling holes for homemade marbles or small round stones. Not only were checkers and tic-tac-toe played, but also a game called Nine Men's Moves (similar to Chinese checkers), in which two players maneuvered their men for position. Fox and Geese was another popular board game, in which 24 marbles, representing the geese, moved against two other marbles—the foxes. Other games made from wood included quoits, pill-in-the-bottle, peg-in-the-hole, and chess.

Wooden blocks for creating villages, houses, and farms provided hours of entertainment, as did spool racers, paddlewheelers, and pull horses. One of the favorite toys was the rocking horse made from a log or a piece of wood. These home-crafted broncos kicked up the dust in many pioneer homes as they rocked to and fro for many miles of adventure. A cowhide bridle kept the horse's swift gallop in check.

Other wooden toys included doll cradles, beds, tables, chairs, and other play furniture, as well as doll houses, many of which were rather ornate and detailed.

The pioneers, ever concerned for the education of their children, combined learning with fun in such devices as wooden slate boards, often with the alphabet carved into the surface, and counting boards fashioned like an abacus.

Wooden whistles, flutes, and toy musical instruments were also popular with pioneer children. Any boy worth his salt could make a willow whistle, and whittling became a favorite pastime not only of young boys, but of older men as well. It took many hours of careful, skillful cutting to create some of the beautifully carved toys, such as whirligigs and climbing bears. Those few that have survived are museum pieces today.

Today's flimsy plastic toys that are broken and forgotten after a few hours are poor substitutes for the sturdy toys of yesterday. Modern parents searching for children's

playthings that are durable, challenging, and satisfying might do well to duplicate the skills of their grandparents either by providing the materials for constructing good toys or by making the toys with the same dedication and interest as pioneer parents.

PIONEER DOLLS

Pioneer doll making had three dimensions. One of these was the production of dolls as toys or playthings for children; another was doll making as a spontaneous expression of traditional folk art; and the third was making a personal or aesthetic statement with dolls in an effort to communicate with others.

As folk art, pioneer dolls continued a well-established tradition, because the pioneer artists, through doll making, expressed themselves in an unassuming and sometimes naive way. As in any art form, the ultimate value of the work depended upon the perceptive abilities of the artist, unhampered by artificial rules or stereotyped styles.

Dolls for pioneer children had to be made at home from the materials at hand, including scraps of cloth; wool; bits of lace; shreds of materials used for stuffing, such as sawdust, bran, or cotton batting; cords; twine, string; wood; pine cones; cornhusks; corncobs; walnuts and other kinds of nuts; flowers; seeds and pods; leather, and other gifts of nature.

Some of the earliest dolls that have been

preserved because of the sturdiness of their construction include wooden dolls and dolls made of nuts or corncobs. Dolls made from fabric, rags, or yarn were not so durable, and not many of these survive. Pioneer children, like children of all ages, played with and enjoyed their dolls till the dolls wore out from sheer loving care or, more rarely, from carelessness.

Doughnut Dolls

One of the earliest and certainly the most fragile of the pioneer dolls was the doughnut or fried cake doll. When early pioneer parents and grandparents found themselves involved in the almost universal problem of providing some kind of satisfactory doll for their little girl's Christmas stocking, they were forced to be truly ingenious and resourceful. One of the earliest and most dearly loved dolls was made of doughnut batter or dough that was rolled out, cut in a doll shape, and fried in deep fat. Doughnut dolls were used as a special treat to greet the children on Christmas morning and other holidays and special events.

One diary tells of a pioneer girl and her girl friends who *"joyously wrapped up their 'dollies,' sang to them, took them visiting, played house with them, and enjoyed them thoroughly until other interests claimed their attention. Because food was so precious the ultimate end was inevitable in spite of . . . accumulations from grimy hands. But there was no grief or regrets and the little bereft 'mothers' still loved the memories of* their welcome short-lived [dolls]." (Annie C. Kimball, in *Treasures of Pioneer History*, vol. 2, p. 185.)

A much-loved doll was the gingerbread doll, made from aromatic, spicy dough. This doll gave intense, if fleeting, pleasure to the child, appealing to the senses of sight and smell and taste. The really delicious pioneer recipe for making gingerbread dolls that follows is reminiscent of the traditions of baking that many of the pioneers brought with them from Europe.

Pioneer Gingerbread Doll

1 cup dark brown sugar
3 tablespoons milk
3 cups flour
¾ teaspoon ginger
1½ teaspoons cloves
1½ teaspoons cinnamon
¾ teaspoon nutmeg
⅛ teaspoon baking powder
⅛ teaspoon salt
1¼ cups butter

Prepare the dough the day before it is to be baked. In a small bowl combine brown sugar and milk; stir until smooth. Into a large bowl sift the dry ingredients. Using two knives, cut the butter into the dry ingredients until it has the texture of cornmeal. Add the brown sugar and milk mixture and mix well. Wrap dough in wax paper or cover with a damp cloth, and chill. Heat oven to 350° F. Roll out dough on a floured table or board and cut with sharp knife or cookie cutter into gingerbread doll shape. Place on greased baking tin and bake for 10-12 minutes until lightly browned. Before baking, raisins, cloves, currants, or cherries may be used for facial features or clothing. Decorate dolls with frosting, if desired.

Rag Dolls

The rag doll gave happiness all the days of its existence. Soft and cuddly, it was the doll that was slept with, hugged, used, played with, neglected for a few days and retrieved again, and it has remained "responsive" regardless of its care or lack of it.

The oldest doll in America, the rag doll was a true folk doll of the United States and a favorite of the frontier family. Like all things that come from the heart of people, it was both common and individual, both many and one. It could be large or small, fat or thin, and dressed with sewed-on removable clothes.

Each doll was made in an amazing fashion from many colors and pieces, from the old rags in a scrap bag, from odds and ends, and from left-overs. One of the earliest of the rag dolls had neither arms nor legs and was often cut out with little sense of proportion, depending on chance and the artistic ability of the maker. Its hair was fashioned out of yarn, cowhide strips, or even human hair, and its face was usually made from old underwear or a discarded stocking cap, with the features embroidered or painted on with berry juice paint or ink. Sometimes in the rush of creative activity the facial features were forgotten.

A story about pioneer rag dolls reveals how precious they were to the children who owned them.

At this Christmas season, [my mother] . . . was in a quandry what to give her two little daughters, Ruth and Margaret, age eight and ten. It was an impossibility to buy dolls, so she conceived the idea of making them each a rag doll. How this could be accomplished without their knowledge, she would have to work out after the children had retired. Each night she and her two older daughters would sew and work, work and sew until the task was finished; the result being two large rag dolls with shoes, stocking, chemise, panties, petticoats and yellow checked dresses.

The stockings were hung from the shelf over the old fireplace and Christmas morning what should greet the eyes of the two little girls, but the dollies hanging out of their stockings. They had hair made of yarn, but no faces. When they took them to show Aunt Silver, . . . she told them she would make them some faces. These turned out to be more caricatures than what the girls had expected. Poor Ruth was very unhappy and endeavored to wash off hers with soap and water, which was an impossibility as the work had been done in ink. While trying to dry it out, she held it in front of the blazing fireplace and it was scorched. I can remember her dismay when she discovered what had happened. Of course, through mother's resourcefulness, the face was restored. There never were any dolls which had more care or fondling, more clothes made for them, more love bestowed upon them than did those two dolls. (Margaret Smith Jensen, in *Treasures of Pioneer History*, vol. 5, pp. 188-89.)

For the amateur dollmaker, the simplest form of rag doll was made of a handerchief, a piece of flannel, a blanket, or any soft cloth. A wad of padding was placed in the center of a square piece of the cloth and tied with a string to suggest a head and body. Sometimes a small section of cloth on either side was wound with string to form arms. The doll was often wrapped in another piece of fabric to form a bunting. Such a doll was fashioned in a few minutes but provided many hours of pleasure and comfort to small children.

Flat unjointed dolls were the next stage in the creation of homemade dolls. A double piece of cloth was cut in a doll shape and sewn together, turned, and stuffed with filling to give it form. Features were drawn on with a pen or paint or embroidered with thread; the hair was sewn on, and the doll was dressed in a simple one-piece dress, often gathered at the neck.

Later on, shaped and jointed dolls—such as the familiar Raggedy Ann doll—were made in much the same fashion as unjointed dolls. They were stitched across at the arm and leg joints as each part was stuffed, to allow the arms and legs to be moved or bent.

Sometimes the arms, legs, and head were added separately to the body of the rag doll, thus providing more flexibility and movement. The different doll parts were cut, sewn, and stuffed separately and then joined together with sturdy stitching. Some dolls were made with even greater detail and had nose, eyes, and ears made separately and attached after the head was stuffed.

Clay Dolls

Few porcelain or bisque dolls found their way across the prairies in covered wagons or handcarts. The space was needed for more important survival goods. But the pioneer mother and child often yearned for a facsimile of those beautiful dolls and used their creative imaginations to produce replicas.

Clay heads could be used instead of porcelain ones, since clay was plentiful, easy to handle, and fun to work with. After the damp clay was shaped into heads, arms, and legs, it was left to dry or bake in the sun. Even a wig could be made from clay, formed around a wooden darning egg and then gently slipped off to dry before it was painted and glued to the head.

The bodies of these dolls were usually made from cloth, leather, or wood. The body parts were securely glued to the body or inserted into holes in the fabric body, with the edges of the material wrapped with string and tied over the clay part. Then the body was stuffed.

Eggshell Heads

A substitute porcelain doll was made by one clever pioneer mother for her small daughter by using an empty eggshell for the head. A small portion of the end of the egg was cut off and the contents removed. The balance of the eggshell was lightly stuffed with scraps of cloth or sawdust, then a piece of fabric with a hole in the center was pulled over the egg-head and glued to the shell. A ribbon tied around the place where the shell and fabric were joined covered the ragged edges. The face was then drawn on with paint and the hair pasted on.

Porcelain Heads

One fortunate pioneer girl related the joy she had with the doll her mother made for her one Christmas:

My clever, thoughtful mother made the body of strong new Indian Head factory muslin and sewed on the beautiful china head. The body was large—the largest doll I had ever seen. Instead of stuffing it with the sawdust or bran, patient hands had cut old, soft cloth scraps, which as filling, made the body firm, yet soft. Seams at knees and elbows made flexible limbs which were sewed to the

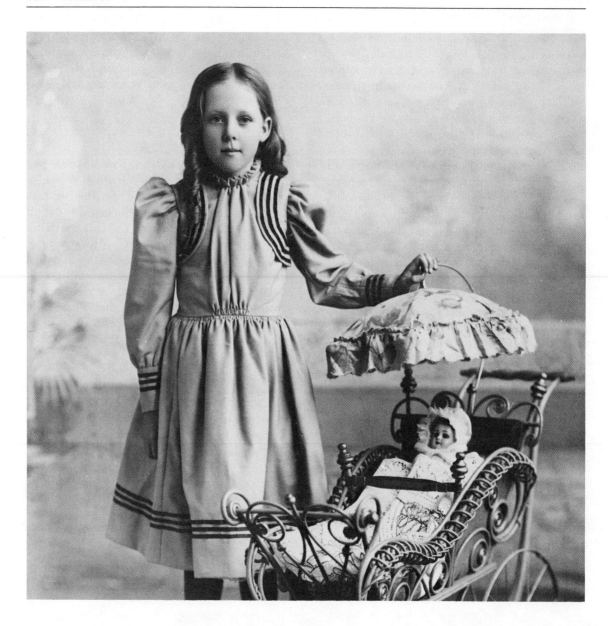

torso. Although the expression on the pleasant face was that of a child from four to six, yet when she was dressed in her long baby dresses and petticoats of that period with a properly pinned diaper and a real baby-wrap blanket, she immediately became an infant in natural size and feel. (Kimball, *Treasures of Pioneer History,* vol. 5, pp. 186-87.)

Wooden Dolls

Other early dolls were those made from pieces of wood. During the earliest period of pioneer life the crudely carved wooden dolls were seen only occasionally, because they took too many precious hours to make. Sometimes they were very roughly made, but often they were carved or whittled with the greatest of care. Even the crudest and simplest dolls were transformed by the magic of make-believe and provided hours of enchanted play for the lonely pioneer boy or girl.

One favorite wooden doll was made from a single piece of jack-pine, carefully whittled or carved into a rough cylinder. Hair was painted on, or a piece of raveled fabric was glued in place, or a pine-cone was fastened on for a fine topknot. Facial features were painted on or were made by gluing on seeds for the eyes, nose, and mouth. Twigs were attached for arms, and small shirts or shawls were fashioned from scraps.

The following story relates how two pioneer children became the proud possessors of wooden dolls after their father became known as a peacemaker among the Indians:

One day he purchased from them for a sack of corn two wonderfully carved wooden, painted dolls, each as large as a baby. They seemed so beautiful to these little pioneer girls, Dora and Lauretta, that they played with them continuously from morning until night.... Consequently the floors were unswept and the dishes unwashed. This unpardonable neglect was more than their immaculate Welsh mother could stand, so she threw both dolls into the fire. Being too tall to burn all at once, the legs dangled out in front of the stove. Little Dora never forgot the heartbreak she felt as she watched the dolls burn and even to her old age this sad memory was one of the major tragedies of her life. (Kimball, *Treasures of Pioneer History,* vol. 5, p. 188.)

Penny Wooden Dolls

Penny wooden dolls were favorites of the frontier children. The doll body and head were carved from a soft wood, such as pine, by the pioneer father and then dressed by an equally skilled mother. They were usually small dolls, not more than a few inches high—just the right size for little hands. Penny dolls could be tucked into a pocket and taken with ease visiting or even to church, and provided many happy hours for make-believe mothers.

Darning Egg Doll

Wooden darning eggs from mother's mend-

ing basket made satisfactory substitute dolls in the absence of more conventional ones. The wooden egg formed the head, and the body or clothes were made by tying fabric around the wooden handle. A matching bonnet of calico was tied over the head to frame the face. Facial features were not necessary for this doll, which had a distinctive personality of its own.

Clothespin Dolls

Clothespin dolls, small like the penny dolls, were fashioned from wooden clothespins, which in pioneer times were all homemade. The shape of the clothespins provided the ready-made head and legs. Facial features were painted on the round ball at the top of the pin with a pencil or ink. The body was draped in a small piece of cloth fastened tightly to the neck of the clothespin, with the legs formed naturally by the two pins. The feet could be sanded off so the doll would stand or they were fastened to a base.

Cornhusk Dolls

The only native rivals to the rag doll in pioneer homes were dolls made of cornhusks and corncobs. Although they were made from the most primitive of materials, they often looked like fashionable ladies with bonnets and parasols. Some have survived and can be seen in pioneer museums. These popular dolls were made by the Indians as well as the pioneers. They were made of soft, pliable cornhusks, which were soaked or even simmered in hot water. Then they were drained and formed while damp but not dripping. (If green husks were used, they were first spread out to dry in a warm dry place to avoid mildew. If dried indoors, they retained their soft green color. If another color was desired, a vegetable dye was added to the hot water.)

When the husks were ready, a small piece of husk was rolled into a ball for the head, and a larger ball was formed for the upper part of the body. The two balls were fastened together with string or raffia.

A flat piece of husk was placed over the two balls from front to back, with the piece twisted once at the top of the head to hold it neatly. A string was tied between the two balls to form the neck, and the figure was also tied firmly at the waistline. A skirt was made from several thicknesses of corn husks, tied to the upper body at the waist, and trimmed evenly at the bottom.

Arms were formed from narrow strands of husks tied at the wrist and fastened to the body. The face was simply painted on. Hair was formed from wet corn silk or from corn husks braided and pinned in place. For braided hair, the husks were torn into narrow strips, soaked, tied in groups of three or more strands, and braided to the desired length.

Bonnets, pinafores, baby dolls, parasols, and other accessories were fashioned from other wet corn husks.

To make a baby doll, a tiny ball of husk (about one-fourth inch in diameter) was

rolled up, covered with a smooth husk as for the larger doll, and tied with string at the neck, to form the doll's head and dress. A piece of husk three-fourths-inch wide was tied over the head for a bonnet. Facial features were a small circle for a mouth and two dots for eyes.

Yarn Dolls

Scraps of yarn from mother's or grandmother's knitting basket provided the material for soft, cuddly dolls. They had a floppiness and softness that made them fun to hold, to hug, to love, and to sleep with, and they were so easy to make that children could do them. Yarn was wound to make many strands. These were tied with a small piece of string, and the yarn was cut opposite the string, to make the strands. The strands were then tied off to form body, arms, and legs. Sometimes the dolls were wrapped in a flannel blanket or dressed in knitted clothes or clothes made from the scrap cloth.

Apple Dolls

The famous dried apple doll was adapted from dolls made by Indians. It was natural for the pioneer mother to find the charm and easy construction of these dolls suitable for her own children. Creating marvelous old characters with life-like features was a favorite occupation of many families.

Instructions for making the apple dolls have not changed since pioneer times. Medium-sized apples of any kind were used. (Winesaps or Baldwins made good dolls.) The apple was carefully peeled and the shape of the head determined by the shape of the apple, usually tapering toward the bottom with the fullness of the apple at the top. The apple was smoothed with a knife, and the facial features were cut deep into the apple. Each apple dried differently, though they were cut the same way, so the features were cut a little larger than desired because the drying process shrank them somewhat. Triangular cuts were made for the eyes, with slits above to form the brows. After the nose was cut, cheeks were shaped and a small groove was cut under the chin. Grooves were also cut at the side to form ears. To make wrinkles, the apple face was sometimes scored with a thumbnail across the forehead, cheeks, and chin, but usually wrinkles appeared naturally as the apple dried. Small nails or seeds were glued into the eyes to give them expression. The apple was placed in a warm place—on the fireplace mantelpiece or a sunny windowsill—to dry thoroughly. This took about three weeks. As the apple dried, the features were pinched periodically to shape the face.

When the head was completely dry, a stick for the body was pushed into it and dressed, or the apple head was attached to a prepared body. Sometimes the body made with a wire form, then padded with cotton or felt strips. Small balls of damp clay were fastened to the ends of the sticks or wires to form legs and arms. Hands and feet were made from clay or stuffed felt.

When the body was finished, it was dressed in typical pioneer clothes: long dress, sunbonnet, and apron for female dolls and shirt and trousers or overalls for male dolls.

Sock Dolls

The sock doll was easy to make, cast off stockings providing a wide range of color and knits. The foot of the sock was used for the head and body of the doll. The body was stuffed, then tied at the neck and feet. No arms or legs were added to the simplest dolls; they were just soft wads. Yarn hair, button or embroidered eyes, and other facial details were added to the head.

A more detailed doll used the ribbed portion of the sock for a cap and the arms. The toe of the sock became the head of the doll when it was stuffed and tied off. The heel of the sock made the "seat" of the doll so it could sit upright. A slit was made in the sock at the open end to form the legs. Then the body and legs were stuffed and sewn shut. The ribbed portion was cut in half horizontally, with the top half used for a cap for the doll. The rest of the ribbed edge was cut into two parts, sewn, and stuffed to make arms, which were sewn to the body. The facial features and clothes were added last.

Hollyhock Dolls

Pioneer children made dolls from whatever materials they could find in nature. They fabricated figures from potatoes, carrots, and gourds; from an acorn, a walnut, a filbert; or from flowers and blossoms. Out of nature's bounty came an assortment of perishable and fragile dolls.

Of these dolls, none captured the hearts of the children more than hollyhock dolls. In almost every pioneer garden the stately, hardy, old-fashioned hollyhock flourished and brought gay colors to the summer landscape. Ruffled blossoms in bright shades of red, pink, yellow, rose, and lavender, as well as white, made exquisite dolls for the children who loved their soft beauty.

To construct the dolls, hollyhock blossoms and a bud were fastened together with small wooden twigs or pins to form a bodice. Sometimes another blossom was fastened to a long stick to make a parasol, or a small blossom placed on the head for a hat. Though these dolls had a short lifespan, lasting no longer than part of a day, they provided a bit of elegance and charm to the children's rather austere lives.

The charm of the hollyhock doll is recalled in a verse of poetry called "Yesteryears," written by pioneer child who loved these charming dolls as had her mother and grandmother before her. She asks:

> *Did you ever make a hollyhock doll*
> *With a green grape pinned on for a head?*
> *They made such beautiful little girls*
> *With their dresses of yellow and red.*[1]

In answer to her question, almost every little pioneer girl could say yes.

[1]Annie A. Tanner, *My Shining Valley* (Brigham Young University Press, 1974), p. 23.

BIBLIOGRAPHY

Atwater, Mary. *The Shuttlecraft Book of American Hand Weaving.* New York: The Macmillan Co., 1951.

Birrell, Verla. *The Textile Arts.* New York: Harper & Row, 1959.

Bowles, Ella S. *Handmade Rugs.* Boston: Little, Brown & Co., 1927.

Carter, Kate B. (comp.). *Heart Throbs of the West.* 12 vols. Salt Lake City: Daughters of Utah Pioneers, 1940-51.

Carter, Kate B. (comp.). *Treasures of Pioneer History.* 6 vols. Salt Lake City: Daughters of Utah Pioneers, 1952-62.

Fannie Farmer Cookbook. New York: Crown Publishing Inc., 1896.

Harmer, Mabel. *The Story of the Mormon Pioneers.* Salt Lake City: Deseret Press, 1943.

Jardine, Winnifred. *Famous Mormon Recipes.* Salt Lake City: Liddle Enterprises, 1972.

Journal of Discourses. 26 vols. Salt Lake City: Deseret News Press, 1966.

Lamprecht, Helen. "Textile Arts of the Mormon Pioneers." Unpublished master's thesis, Oregon State University, 1965.

Leach, Alma. *Vegetable Dyeing.* New York: Watson Guptill Publications, Inc., 1956.

Miller, Albert E. *The Immortal Pioneers, Founders of St. George, Utah.* St. George, Utah, 1946.

Tanner, Annie Clark. *A Mormon Mother.* Salt Lake City: University of Utah Library, 1969.

Wiggington, Eliot (ed.). *Foxfire.* Garden City, N.Y.: Anchor Press, 1972.

Books on Needlepoint

Gartner, Louis J., Jr. *Needlepoint Design.* New York: William Morrow & Co., 1970.

Haraszty, Eszter, and Bruce D. Colen. *Needlepointing: A Garden of Stitches.* New York: Liveright, 1974.

Katzenberg, Gloria. *Needlepoint and Pattern: Themes and Variations.* New York: The Macmillan Co., 1974.

Orr, Jan. *Now Needlepoint.* New York: Van Nostrand Reinhold, 1975.

Parker, Xenia L. *A Beginner's Book of Needlepoint and Embroidery.* New York: Dodd, Mead & Co., 1975.

Tillett, Leslie. *American Needlework: 1776/1976.* New York: New York Graphic Society, 1975.

Weal, Michele. *Texture and Color in Needlepoint.* New York: Harper & Row, 1975.

Knitting and Crocheting

Cone, Ferne. *Knit Art.* New York: Van Nostrand Reinhold Co., 1975.

Sommer, Elyse. *A New Look at Crochet.* New York: Crown Publishers, 1975.

Ventre, Mary T. *Crochet.* New York: Little, Brown & Co., 1974.

Embroidery

Frew, Hannah. *Three-Dimensional Embroidery.* New York: Van Nostrand Reinhold, 1975.

Gostelow, Mary. *A World of Embroidery.* New York: Charles Scribner's Sons, 1975.

Muelenbelt-Neiuwburg, Alberta. *Embroidery Designs from Old Dutch Samplers.* New York: Charles Scribner's Sons, 1975.

Nichols, Marion (ed.). *Designs and Patterns for*

Embroiderers and Craftsmen. New York: Dover Publishing, Inc., 1974.

Rosse, Allianora. *Flower Embroidery.* New York: Charles Scribner's Sons, 1974.

Quilting

Houck, Carter, and Myron Miller. *American Quilts and How to Make Them.* New York: Charles Scribner's Sons, 1975.

Jarnow, Jill. *The Patchwork Point of View.* New York: Simon and Schuster, 1975.

Newman, Thelma R. *Quilting, Patchwork, Applique, and Trapunto.* New York: Crown Publishing Inc., 1974.

Weaving and Rug Making

Cuyler, Susanna. *The High-Pile Rug Book.* New York: Harper & Row, 1974.

Felcher, Cecilia. *The Complete Book of Rug Making.* New York: Hawthorn, 1975.

Moshimer, Joan. *The Complete Rug Hooker: The Craft and the Tradition.* New York: New York Graphic Society, 1975.

Russell, Elfleda. *Off-Loom Weaving.* New York: Little, Brown & Co., 1975.

Miscellaneous Craft Books

Blue Mountain Crafts Council. *The Joy of Crafts.* New York: Holt, Rinehart & Winston, 1975.

Fiarotta, Phyllis. *Phyllis Fiarotta's Nostalgia Crafts Book.* New York: Workman Publishing Co., 1975.

Johnson, Jann. *Jann Johnson's Discovery Book of Crafts.* Pleasantville, N.Y.: Reader's Digest Press, 1975.

Sandford, Lettice. *Straw Work and Corn Dollies.* New York: Viking Press, Inc., 1975.

Schutz, Walter E. *How to Make Wooden Toys and Games.* New York: The Macmillan Co., 1975.

Shipman, Dorothy, and Moyna McWilliam. *Everlasting Flowercraft.* New York: Arco Publishing Co., Inc., 1975.

Crafts Supplies Sources, References, and How-To Information

Boyd, Margaret A. *The Mail Order Crafts Catalogue.* New York: Chilton Book Co., 1975.

Glassman, Judith. *National Guide to Crafts Supplies.* New York: Van Nostrand Reinhold, 1975.

Lippman, Deborah, and Paul Colin. *Handmade: A Catalog of Craft Resources.* Philadelphia: M. Evans & Co., 1975.

Shields, Joyce F. *Make It: An Index to Projects and Materials.* Metuchen, N. J.: Scarecrow Press, 1975.

INDEX